West European Business and Social Etiquette

a smart guide toward successful business

Dr. Kathy S. ten Broeke

AuthorHouse™
1663 Liberty Drive, Suite 200
Bloomington, IN 47403
www.authorhouse.com
Phone: 1-800-839-8640

AuthorHouse™ UK Ltd.
500 Avebury Boulevard
Central Milton Keynes, MK9 2BE
www.authorhouse.co.uk
Phone: 08001974150

© 2006 Kathy S. ten Broeke. All rights reserved.

No part of this publication may be reproduced, stored or introduced into a retrieval system, or likewise copied in any form, without the prior written permission of the author, excepting quotes for review or citation.

First published by AuthorHouse 8/18/2006

ISBN: 1-4259-5176-7

Printed in the United States of America
Bloomington, Indiana

This book is printed on acid-free paper.

The data and recommendations in this book are based on extensive research and experience over many years by the author. The author and/or publishing company cannot be held liable for any errors or omissions and cannot be held responsible for how the reader chooses to use this information.

Bloomington, IN  Milton Keynes, UK

West European Business and Social Etiquette
a smart guide toward successful business

Introduction

Ignorance may cause very uncomfortable situations, missed opportunities, or even embarrassment. To avoid all of that, while doing business in western Europe, some useful guidelines will tell you how to behave the proper way according to the local or national etiquette of the places and countries in which you are doing business. Etiquette varies by country and even by region in western Europe, but there are general guidelines that help make you feel more at ease while doing business or when socializing.

When you treat people with respect and you behave in a correct way, you create a pleasant atmosphere, whether it concerns a business environment or a social one. That is what it is all about: respect the people around you and try to adjust as much as possible when you are a guest in another country.

However, always expect the unexpected.

Hereafter you'll find guidelines regarding major topics in business, from the first meeting until the deal is closed and everything in between. In order to become successful you will be instructed:

 and

what you should do   and   what you should not do.

Apart from all the guidelines, you will find some interesting tips about specific situations that might help you to meet the needs of your business counterparts. Also some useful checklists on specific business situations such as preparing presentations, agendas, and pointers on how to tackle specific behavior, will guide you along the way toward doing business successfully. The anecdotes about some embarrassing situations may even put a smile on your face.

West European Business and Social Etiquette

Contents

Chapter	page

PART ONE

Introduction — i

1 Brief History of West European Etiquette — 1
 1.1 First rules — 1
 1.2 Basic principles — 1

2 First Business Meetings — 3
 2.1 Dress, shake, look, state — 3
 2.2 Observe and identify your business counterpart — 3
 2.3 Language barrier — 4

3 General Guidelines for Business Etiquette — 6
 3.1 First business meetings, appointments — 6
 3.2 Dress code — 6
 3.3 Addressing people — 6
 3.4 Business cards — 6
 3.5 Incentives — 7
 3.6 Doing business — 7
 3.7 Business meals — 7

4 General Guidelines for Proper Table Manners — 9
 4.1 The napkin — 9
 4.2 Handling silverware — 10
 4.3 Handling tableware — 11
 4.4 Glasses, water and wine — 12
 4.5 Fingerbowl — 13

5 General Guidelines for Social Etiquette — 14

West European Business and Social Etiquette

Contents

Chapter	page
PART TWO	
17 West European countries	
01 Iceland	**17**
02 Norway	**23**
03 Sweden	**29**
04 Finland	**35**
05 Denmark	**41**
06 United Kingdom	**47**
07 Ireland	**53**
08 the Netherlands	**59**
09 Belgium	**65**
10 Luxembourg	**71**
11 Germany	**77**
12 Austria	**83**
13 Switzerland	**89**
14 France	**95**
15 Italy	**101**
16 Spain	**107**
17 Portugal	**113**
Bibliography	128

1
Brief History of West European Etiquette

1.1 First Rules

The first known written rules about etiquette date back to the year 2300 B.C., written on papyrus by Ptah-Hotep, an Egyptian priest, or landlord, whose wisdom survived the eras. He wrote these rules down for his son who apparently refused to behave nicely. In Europe the first book about etiquette was written around 1475 by the usher of Lord Charles the Bold in the Netherlands. It dealt mainly with table manners. The origins of today's etiquette, however, began in the French royal courts in the 1600s and 1700s. Under King Louis XIV, a placard was devised and posted with rules for everybody to obey. The word etiquette means, literally, ticket, card or placard.

Some of those rules were
- don't put food back on the serving dish after you have taken a bite from it;
- don't pet dogs and cats during dinner;
- make sure your hands and nails are clean;
- don't scratch your head;
- don't lick your plate clean;
- don't wipe your greasy hands on the table cloth;
- avoid making disturbing bodily noises.

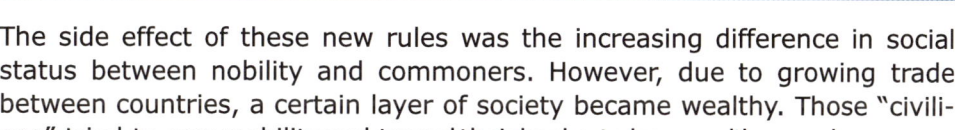

The side effect of these new rules was the increasing difference in social status between nobility and commoners. However, due to growing trade between countries, a certain layer of society became wealthy. Those "civilians" tried to copy nobility and turned their backs to less-wealthy people.

In countries with difference in social status, etiquette is very important. In countries where the social layers of the population are not very clear, you will find fewer etiquette rules. Etiquette is very important where royalty still rules, especially in countries such as Sweden, Denmark, Norway, England, Belgium, and the Netherlands.

Countries where royalty has disappeared, e.g., France, Germany, Italy and Portugal have different etiquette in social behavior; showing good table manners, however, is imperative for all of western Europe.

1.2 Basic Principles

Due to changing times, etiquette has changed somewhat as well. Try to see etiquette as a package of flexible guidelines, there to help you to adjust to your surroundings. The main principle has remained the same through the ages: **respecting each other**.

Respect the fact that people can be totally different from you. Treat people the way you like to be treated. You don't have to feel threatened by situations in which you don't know what to do. Try to interpret the situation, and act accordingly, while showing respectful behavior.

By the way, showing good manners doesn't necessarily mean that the person performing, is as good as his manners. On the contrary, even when a person hasn't been educated in etiquette and never has had a chance to learn about it, he or she can be the best and most reliable person ever.

As for slick-operating individuals, with all their good manners and courteous behavior, sometimes they turn out to be absolutely unreliable people.

2
First Business Encounters

2.1 Dress, Shake, Look, State

Try to adjust the way you **dress**. Europeans like to be dressed formally when in their business mode. Depending on the country, you will find people dressed in either designer fashions or in simply plain, but formal clothing.

First impressions are precious and a one-time-only chance. People judge by what they see, hear, and feel. Therefore, it is advisable to dress your face with a nice smile and the rest of your body in proper, clean clothes.

When handshakes are appropriate, **shake** with a firm "dry" grip, but don't squeeze and don't hold on longer than two seconds.

Look people in the eyes, but **don't stare**.

When introductions are being exchanged, make sure you **state** your name clearly, and try to remember the name of your counterpart. Don't speak with a loud voice; be modest and use a neutral tone of voice. If by chance you didn't hear a name clearly, it's okay to ask your counterpart to repeat his or her name.

2.2 Observe and Identify Your Business Counterpart

It is important that you are able to identify the *type* of person with whom you are dealing with. There are three main types of businesspersons: **the dominant ones, the social ones, and the detached ones**.

Dominant people usually show imperative behavior; they don't ask but command. They are sensitive about their status and appearance and like to have the "last word." You will find a lot of them in Germany and France. Dealing with those persons means, you should listen very closely, show respect, and, most important

- don't try to socialize;
- don't show the same behavior;
- stay friendly;
- keep it "strictly business."

You recognize the dominant ones by observing their attitude when they walk (*firm steps*), their gestures (*imperative*), and their tone of voice and facial expressions (even if you don't understand the language). Dominant people like to stare straight into your eyes, to intimidate and make you feel humble.

Social people show a lot of spontaneous behavior; they like to talk a lot, and they are a bit unpredictable, because they like everybody to be their friend. They like to do business the pleasant way and will spend more time entertaining you than doing business.

You may choose to behave the same way, but remain correct, keep business on track, and try to wrap things up when necessary. You will recognize the social ones by
- *their loose attitude;*
- *friendly smiles;*
- *most of all, by the way they talk to you.*

They will be more interested in you as a person and a little less in your business.

Detached ones don't talk much, and when they do, it will be in short sentences. They hardly look you in the eye; they are very critical and expect everything to be prepared well. They like to live by rules and regulations.

Dealing with them means: you will have to be "strictly business." Don't try a joke or a personal remark; they might feel offended if you do so.
You recognize them by
- their *rigid body language;*
- *usually their hands are clasped together;*
- *arms crossed in front of their chest;*
- *they talk "facts."*

> **TIP**
> **Especially when you are dealing with dominant or detached persons, it sometimes helps to loosen them up a bit, by <u>copying their body language,</u> meaning**
>
> - **sit like they sit;**
> - **move your hands like they do;**
> - **lean on the table when they do, etc.**
>
> **But make sure your copying is inconspicuous.**

2.3 Language Barrier

Doing business with the inhabitants of a foreign country usually means you don't speak their language as well as your own, or even not at all.

Even though your English, French, Spanish or German may be very good, there will be moments in which you might misinterpret a sentence or remark or even a word.

Even more difficult is a situation in which two business partners are being forced to speak a language other than their own. For instance, when a Swede negotiates with a Chinese person, most likely they will speak English. The fact is, they will speak English as they have been taught, and this will carry a lot of their own "tongue" in it, which causes one to be misunderstood by the other.

> **TIP**
> If your business counterpart tells you something about the terms of a contract, or maybe a delivery and you are not quite sure what he means, here is what you can do
> - first, tell him that you heard him but don't understand him completely;
> - then tell him what you think he meant and ask him to give definitions of the words in the remark;
> - then compare your definitions or interpretations to his.
>
> Be always polite, even if you are asking for the smallest thing. Europeans prefer to be verbally polite, no matter what.

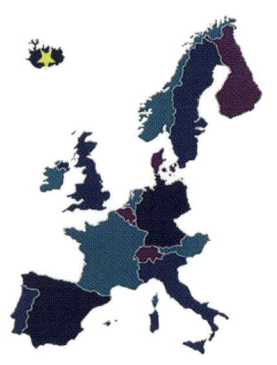

3

General Guidelines for Business Etiquette

3.1 First Business Meetings, Appointments

European businesspeople usually try to be as efficient as possible. Time is money, and in most of the countries that is very true. If you want to make an appointment, it is advisable that you do so in advance, meaning a few weeks ahead, to give your counterparts a chance to prepare for the meeting. Nowadays electronics make communication easy and very fast. Most of the arrangements will travel through the digital medium, but do make hard copies of agreements. Print important e-mails and bring them with you. Do pay attention to the following: **Europeans write the day first, then the month and the year, e.g., June 25, 2008, is written as 25-06-2008, or sometimes 25 June, 2008.**

3.2 Dress Code

Looking clean and well dressed, is what one expects in western Europe. Rather than wearing bright colors or flashy outfits (designer or not), people like to see you dressed in a formal but nice-looking outfit. Even though you see more often that businesses allow their employees to have a **"casual Friday,"** they don't really expect you to show up casually dressed for a business meeting.

3.3 Addressing People

In some countries, it is perfectly normal to address each other on a first-name basis. However, in other countries, people insist on being addressed by their family name and full title. See the specific country, in order to find out about the proper way of addressing people.

3.4 Business Cards

Of course, bring plenty of business cards. You might find yourself in a situation, in which you meet more important people than you had expected. When meeting for the first time, the first thing you do, is exchange cards. Don't just put them in your pocket, without even looking at them. That is a sign of disrespect. Take a minute to review the card and maybe even compliment the giver on it.

> **TIP**
> In case you get a few cards at the same time, it might come in handy to place them in front of you in the same order in which people are sitting at the table, so you will know who is who.

In some countries people expect you to have translated (and even specially made) your cards for them, so that they can understand what your title is. Check the specific countries on that topic.

3.5 Incentives
Giving incentives can be very tricky. In some countries people see it as a bribe; in other countries they expect it from you, and there are countries in which people want to give **YOU** an incentive as a token of friendship, and the start of doing business in a pleasant way. For that matter, you'd better check the listed country and decide accordingly.

3.6 Doing Business
Due to the multinational population of some countries, it is very hard to give specific guidelines for doing business. However, it does not only depend on good manners and respect, even though they can be the key to your success. Sometimes you have to have more tools present to tackle business. **Identifying** your counterpart is one of the tools, but there are many more.

It is also hard to predict what type of negotiating skills people use in a country. Check the Internet on this topic. Let it be clear that whatever is transpiring during a meeting, the best thing for you to do is, to **resume** all important topics and **verify** with the others whether you have understood everything in the way they have meant it.

3.7 Business Meals
It is commonly accepted that most deals will be closed during a nice business meal. Depending on the type of deal and the moment of closure, you might attend either a lunch or a dinner. It is most important to know how to **behave properly** during these events.

Lunch
A business lunch is meant to create an atmosphere of mutual trust or comfort with one another. Depending on the country you are in, you'll find different types of business lunches
- a sandwich in the office of the business host;
- going out for a quick sandwich;
- having a sandwich in the office cafeteria;
- a warm lunch in the company's restaurant;
- an extended warm meal somewhere in a nice restaurant.

The last two scenarios are more formal than the first three mentioned, however, in all five scenarios one would expect the conversation to be directed toward business. When dining in the office, it is not rude for you to leave all pertinent documents, files, etc., in your workspace, as they may be necessary during your conversations.

When leaving the office for lunch, you typically are not expected to bring any documents, unless specifically noted to do so. When you are invited for a business lunch, the host will always inform you about the place, either in or outside the office. Therefore, you may have to adjust your **dress code** according to the ruling company culture, but in general you will do fine with a suit or a jacket and a tie.

Cocktail Hour
In some countries it is customary to have cocktails before dinner. Keep in mind that those cocktail hours are not supposed to get you into a higher atmosphere before you start your dinner; they are merely a nice way of socializing before you get down to business.

Dinner
A business dinner is, by all means, meant to do business and to get to know each other, business-wise. You will be invited to go to a restaurant, so make sure you are well dressed. When the waiter knows who the host is, they will give the guests the menu first. When you close your menu or put it back on the table, it means the waiter can come and take your order. Now this can be a bit tricky. If the party is rather small, the host may place all the orders for everybody (after having discussed this with everyone, of course). However, if the party is rather large, then the waiter will take individual orders.

According to proper etiquette, ordering from the menu should follow this sequence: the older ladies first, then the younger ones, then the older men, and then the younger ones. But during a business lunch and/or dinner, most of the time this is not the procedure; usually the guests will order in the sequence of seating and the waiter will address each person individually in that order. The moment the food is being served, you will notice that the guests receive their food first, and then the host.

Note: There are still people who like to say grace (pray) before they have dinner. The host then might ask for a moment of silence for those who want to say grace.

4
General Guidelines for Proper Table Manners

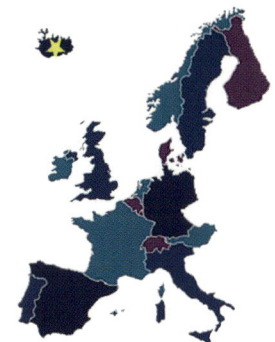

The best guide to proper table manners is your common sense. If you are not sure what to do or how to handle the different "tools," just sit back and wait until your host starts, so you can copy his movements. Try to keep a low profile while eating; don't draw attention to yourself by talking loudly. Let's start with the absolute "no-nos" and thereafter give you the proper way to conduct yourself.

NO-NOS

- Don't start eating before everybody has their food.
- Don't put your napkin between your collar and neck.
- Don't make slurping noises while drinking or eating soup.
- Don't make disgusting sounds while chewing your food.
- Don't chew with your mouth open.
- Don't stuff your mouth.
- Don't overload your fork.
- Don't ever eat from or lick your knife.
- Don't hang over your plate.
- Don't have your elbows on the table.
- Don't spread your arms wide out.
- Don't poke your fingers in your mouth, pick your teeth, etc.
- Don't wash your food down with water or wine.
- Don't put bones etc. back on the serving plate, keep all on your own plate.
- Don't speak while having food in your mouth.
- Don't go to the bathroom while everybody is still eating.
- Don't leave the table without asking permission.

Now this all may seem a bit childish and quite obvious, but in many ways the smallest misbehavior can lead to frowning faces. And you do want to avoid that during important business deals.

4.1 The Napkin
Your napkin is usually situated on the left side of your plate, or sometimes on top of your plate. After you have seated yourself, you take your napkin, fold it either twice or three times (depending on the size), and put it on your lap.

Never tie it around your neck or stuff it in your shirt collar. Don't use it to wipe your face, nor may you use it to clean your silverware or glass(es). If you feel that your silverware or glass is dirty, you should ask the waiter for clean replacements.

The napkin is there to protect your clothes, so put it on your lap. You may use it to wipe your fingers and also, with the corners, to wipe your mouth. Use the inside of the folded napkin to wipe the corners of your mouth in order to prevent the "grease" from smearing on your clothes.

When you have a fingerbowl next to your plate, first use it to rinse your fingertips, and after that dry your fingers using your napkin. Never make a mess of your napkin, but fold it nicely two or three times and place it at the left side of your plate when you are ready. If you have to leave your seat during the dinner, for whatever reason, place your napkin next to your plate on the left side, nicely folded, with the clean side up.

4.2 Handling Silverware

Don't panic when you see a whole lot of silverware next to your plate. Always start using them from the outside, working your way toward the inside, until you've reached your plate. Silverware lies in the sequence the dishes will be served. The stem of the silverware will be facing the hand it is meant to be used with.

There will never be more silverware than dishes. In other words, use the outermost fork and knife for your appetizer, then the spoon for your soup, and so on and so forth. By the way, in Europe people use **both hands** when handling silverware (except when eating soup). Using only a fork is an absolute no-no. The fork goes into your left hand, and the knife into your right hand, unless you are left-handed, of course.

After using your knife, do not then switch your fork into your right hand and put the knife down (or vice-versa if you are left-handed). Use your righthand to hold the spoon, and ladle the soup away from you, never toward you. And don't lift your plate or bowl to get the last drop out of there. Tiny soup bowls allow you to drink from them, after you have first ladled out the biggest part. One other thing: you always must have both hands on the table, but never your elbows.

In some cases you might get a change of silverware when you have ordered fish. Finer restaurants do set their tables with silverware for fish. The knives are not as sharp and the forks have a specific shape.

Fish meat is NEVER to be cut, but rather to be parted and gently moved toward the fork.

The silverware for the dessert will be above the plate. There will be more silverware above the plate if there are more desserts, such as cheeses, sweets, etc. Dessert silverware should be used from the top down.

Signaling with Silverware

There may be an instance in which you will need to stop eating for a while during the dinner (i.e., someone is making a speech, reading minutes, etc.) or you want to take a small break. In order to prevent the waiter from taking your food, you can show him not to take your plate by signaling with your silverware like this: put your knife and fork across your plate, making sure that the fork crosses the knife.

Now the waiter knows he cannot remove your plate, and in some cases, if he is really well trained, he might come up to you and ask you, if you would like to have more food. But if you don't feel like having more food, and you in fact, want the waiter to take your plate away, you can also signal with your silverware.

Put your knife and fork together, the stems diagonal toward the right side of your plate, the knife on top of the fork with the sharp side toward you and the fork with the teeth down. Now the (well-trained) waiter will come to you and take your plate away.

4.3 Handling Tableware

Plates

Occasionally you will find that the table is already set with large plates. Those are used as the "chargers"; in other words, the waiters will place the plates with food on top of these plates. However, this may vary with the restaurant. It is nice to help the waiter clean up after every course, but it is not necessary, so don't stack the plates. You may hand them to the waiter in case he can't reach them very easily.

When your food is being served, you will notice that the waiter places the plate facing you in a specific way. This is meant to show you how to start eating. Don't mix the different foods into an unrecognizable substance, but try to keep your plate nice and neat while eating.

Bread Plate
You will find the small bread plate at the left side of your plate, and in many cases it has a small butter knife on top of it as well. The butter is mostly put in a small jar on the table with a small butter knife as well. Here is what you do
- take a piece of butter from the jar with its butter knife and put it on your bread plate;
- put the butter knife back on the jar;
- take your own butter knife and use it to put butter on your piece of bread.

When toast is being served, you are allowed to take a bite; when French bread is being served, you may break a piece off of it. The small rolls that are being served, you may eat by hand.

Soup Bowl
Sometimes soup is served in a bowl either with or without "ears." You may tilt the bowl but not lift it. Nor are you supposed to drink from the bowl, unless it is a tiny bowl and it looks more like a cup. These small bowls are often used when turtle soup is being served.

4.4 Glasses, Water and Wine
The glasses are situated at the right side above your plate and also in order of the courses. First you'll see the wine glass to accompany the appetizer, then the one for the main course, etc. Not every restaurant places a water glass on the table, but when it is there, you'll find it usually on top in the middle. Northern Europeans are not big water drinkers, and as written before, it is not customary for you to get water upon arrival in the restaurant. So when you ask for water, you have to specify that you want either ordinary water from the faucet or bottled water with or without "bubbles."

When drinking wine you must be aware of the fact that holding a wine glass has its own rules. **Never cup the glass**; you may spoil the temperature of the wine by doing so. Also **never hold the glass by the foot,** which is only done when tasting wine at official wine-tasting occasions.

You should **hold the glass by the stem**.

TIPS
Here are some tips, just in case you like to show a little bit of knowledge
- with heavy meals you drink heavy wines;
- with light meals, you drink light wines;
- with hearty meals, you drink spicy wines;
- with sweet meals, you drink sweet wines;
- red meat, ask for red wine; white meat, poultry and fish, ask for white wine;
- when drinking several types of wine during a dinner:
  - have the light before the heavy,
  - the dry before the sweet,
  - the white before the red.

In general the smaller wine glasses are used for white wine and the bigger ones for red wine.

Note: Red wine can be refilled, even if there is something still in the glass. White wine however, may never be refilled when there is still wine in the glass. White wine always has a specific temperature and will be kept in a cooler next to or on the table. By adding white wine to the glass, the perfect temperature will be lost because of the mingling of temperatures.

When you don't know your wines, don't pretend to be a connoisseur. There is nothing to be ashamed of. Just let the sommelier advice you, or when the host has a good advice, just go along with his choice.

4.5 Finger Bowl
The little fingerbowl is placed on the top left side of your plate. Mostly it contains some lemon juice and water, or water and a slice of lemon, to rinse the grease from your fingers when you have had finger food, e.g., shrimp, lobster or lamb chops. When you are completely done with your food, rinse your fingers in the little bowl and afterwards dry your fingers using your napkin.

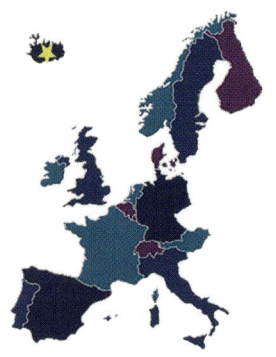

5

General Guidelines for Social Etiquette

People take pride in their country and their region. When it comes to entertaining you as a business guest, and possibly your spouse, you get to know a different side of the country or region and you might be enlightened about their culture, traditions, and art. The beauty of it is that you probably will get to see things that regular tourists will never get to see.

In different countries there are different forms and traditions in entertaining guests. You might have to go to a concert, or visit a museum that you really don't care for. No matter what, just praise the works and express your gratitude. Depending on the type of entertainment, you are to dress according to the situation. Stylishly casual is always acceptable, unless, of course, you are going to the opera or attending a gala.

An invitation to visit the home of one of your business hosts is a possibility. Anticipate a pleasant afternoon or evening. In most countries it is expected that you will bring a gift. You'll find the specific **yes** and **no** gifts under each listed country, as well as topics for conversation. In general, a gift originating from your country will be very welcome, such as photobooks, music, candy, or little souvenirs. It might be a good idea to search the Internet for specific holidays in the country, as well as to look at a map in order to get an idea of the country's situation and the cities you are going to visit.

Also, try to memorize a few words of the native language, just to make a nice impression and to show that you took an interest in the country you are visiting (http://www.word2word.com). Such behavior will be appreciated more than anything. Remember that you are the foreigner and the guest in another country, but don't be afraid to make mistakes, which you can't avoid; after all, you are not expected to know everything and you will be gladly forgiven as long as you show respect.

"Respect" is the magic key word of everything that has to do with business and social etiquette.

- Shake hands with people when you meet them, every time you meet them.
- Look people in the eyes every now and then.
- Wait patiently when you are in line for a service.
- Be polite and always include, please, and/or thank you when you want something or when you receive something.
- When answering a person, use more than just one word: yes sir, or, no madam.
- Dress nicely when you are to appear in public.
- Wash your hands after using the bathroom and before touching food.
- Make sure your nails are clean and your hair is neatly combed.
- Try to smell nice. It is common in western Europe to use mouthwash and deodorant to neutralize possible odors coming from the mouth or body.
- Keep your voice down in public.
- Express gratitude for even the least service rendered to you.
- Compliment people on their country, city, houses, etc.
- Bring small gifts (souvenirs) from your country as incentives.
- Respect women the same as you would respect men.
- Treat women with chivalry; they come first.
- You are expected to ask for clarification, and help when something is not completely clear to you. Europeans are used to people speaking up for themselves.

- Don't keep your hands in your pockets when you talk to someone.
- Don't look away when you have a conversation with someone.
- Don't say just "yes" or "no," when answering a question.
- Don't have chewing gum in your mouth when speaking with someone.
- Don't cut in lines of waiting people.
- Don't speak loudly.
- Don't yawn, burp, or otherwise make bodily noises in public.
- Don't have bad breath.
- Don't scratch yourself or pick your nose while talking to people.
- Don't boast about yourself.
- Don't spread an offensive body odor.
- Don't hesitate to ask for explanations or help.
- Don't be "silent" even if your own culture demands that from you.
- Don't open an umbrella in a house; it means bad luck.

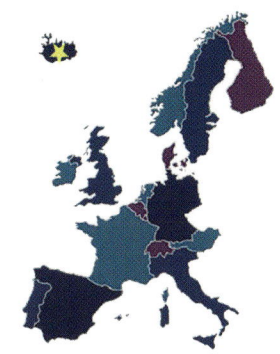

Iceland - ÍSLAND

In General
Iceland is an island, located in the North Atlantic, about 3 hours by air from major cities in western Europe and 5 to 6 hours from the East Coast of the USA. Its mid-Atlantic location makes Iceland an ideal base for companies with businesses on both continents. This Nordic country has active volcanic forces that have created huge resources of geothermal energy. It has a mild climate for its northerly location. The annual temperature in the capital, Reykjavík, is -1 °C in January and +11 °C in July. Iceland is the 12th-largest fishing nation in the world. It is also known for its huge geysers, and many warm (hot) water sulfur wells, where people can bathe all year round. The language is still the same as the language of the Vikings.

A Little History
Iceland was settled in the 9th century by pioneering Vikings on the westward expansion. They founded a unique feudal republic in 930, and the oldest national parliament in the world is still functioning today. Iceland suffered under Norwegian and later Danish (1380) rule, but became a fully independent republic again in 1944.

The 17th and 18th centuries were disastrous for Iceland. English, Spanish, and Algerian pirates raided the coasts and ruined trade; epidemics and volcanic eruptions killed a large part of the population; and the creation (1602) of a private trading company at Copenhagen, with exclusive rights to Iceland trade, caused economic ruin.

The 19th century brought a rebirth of national culture and a desire for independence. In 1874, a constitution and limited home rule were granted; in 1918 Iceland became a sovereign state in personal union with Denmark.

In 1944 a majority of Icelanders voted to terminate the union with Denmark; Iceland became an independent republic on June 17, 1944.
The country is mainly dependant on its fishing industry and behaves therefore very protectively toward its fishing waters. This attitude has led them into many conflicts with Great Britain; one of them even grew into the so-called "Cod Wars" (1972).

Vigdís Finnbogadóttir was elected president in 1980, thus becoming the world's first popularly elected female head of state.

Business Profile

Fishing is the most important industry. Iceland has little heavy industry and relies on imports for many of the necessities of life. The country has diversified its economy and expanded its hydroelectric and geothermal energy resources.

Icelanders can be quite reserved but very upfront. Visitors are often invited into homes, especially if on business. Since even the largest Icelandic corporations are relatively small, you probably find the decision-makers in your first meeting. They are very straightforward and direct, and not only in the business environment. They respect qualities like honesty and being open. Constructive criticism is more appreciated than phony compliments.

Icelanders are proud of their country and like to show you around. Also they like to sing songs about their old, old myths in which bold heroes and their courageous acts come to life again.

"Faux Pas" with Hands

"Once in a **French** company, I already noticed how formal everybody was behaving. Therefore, I tried my best to be as polite and formal as I knew how," said the **Icelandic** importer. "Most of the conversations I had with the management were in the factory, and I talked with them, with one hand in my pocket. I heard them use the words "faux pas" a couple of times, but didn't know what it meant."

Sometimes when people are feeling uncomfortable they tend to hide their hands in their pockets. It is not really a problem when you are attending a social event (though it is still never done when talking to a woman). In business environments it is considered very rude when you have your hands, or even one hand, in your pocket. The French were obviously aware of that fact and maybe said something about it to each other. Faux pas means "false step", so it was a (minor) offense against the rules of etiquette.

First Business Encounters
- Give at least one to three weeks' notice for an appointment.
- Business introductions consist of exchanging cards, names, etc.
- Offer a firm handshake as you make brief eye contact.
- Shake hands with everyone upon coming and going.
- Tell people your first name and family name when being introduced.
- Icelanders like to hear about your trip upon arrival; tell them how it went.

Dress Code
- Check the weather report of the country; it can be cold and rainy.
- Business people are expected to dress smartly. Men wear suit and tie, women wear fashionable suits or skirts.
- Bring formal outfits as well as casual ones.
- Casual attire is allowed in many corporations.
- Bring a sweater or jacket, a raincoat, and a good pair of walking shoes.

Addressing People
- Titles are not all that important.
- First-name basis is very common in business environments.
- Icelandic family names are patronymic; made of the father's first name and the addition of "son" or "dóttir" –daughter-: Olaf Hakaan**son** or Bjork Haralds**dóttir**.
- The telephone directories list people in alphabetical order by first name.

Business Cards
- Bring enough cards.
- Make sure your card is in English and provides your title(s) and position.
- Pay special attention to the cards they give you, so you know who is who, and you also might want to compliment them on theirs.

Incentives
- Bringing a gift is very much appreciated: a bottle of foreign wine, or something nice from your country. Liquor is also always welcome.

Doing Business
- Getting straight down to business is appreciated.
- Business encounters are not formal, but good preparation is important.
- For the first meeting, you need a well-prepared agenda, and a very clear, well-structured presentation.

Business Meals

- Always dress smartly: jacket and tie for men, nice suits for women.
- Lunch and dinner are excellent opportunities for business discussions.
- Business dinners are the preferred form of entertainment.
- Icelanders love to eat and do business at the same time.
- It is advisable to follow the manners and routines of your host, although you don't have to copy his or her drinking pattern.

Table Manners and Etiquette

- All the previous written guidelines are acknowledged in Iceland.

Social Events

- Walking on the street in informal dress is perfectly fine.
- Be punctual at all times, to both business and social events.
- Keep conversation general. Try culture, sports, art, etc., for topics.
- Gifts are the norm for social events. They love chocolates and liquor.
- More-precious gifts are appreciated, when you are staying at a family's house.
- An informal social event, such as a business dinner, still calls for a jacket and tie.
- Expect fun weekends with the Icelanders, but dress for really cold weather.

First Business Encounters
- Do not come late.
- Do not engage in small talk.

Dress Code
- Do not wear casual clothes for business appointments.

Addressing People
- Do not treat any person differently from another.
- Do not forget to shake hands with everyone.

Business Cards
- Do not forget to have your card in English.

Incentives
- Do not forget to bring a gift for the first encounter.

Doing Business
- Do not abruptly change the time and place for appointments.
- Do not show emotions during negotiations.

Business Meals
- Do not start drinking until the host or hostess has proposed a toast to the entire company.
- Do not break eye contact during the toast.
- Do not forget to inform your host about special diets. Icelandic food consists mainly of fish.
- Do not presume to seat yourself.

Table Manners and Etiquette
- All the previously written guidelines still count.

Social Events
- Do not talk about private topics in public.
- Do not hug or kiss or touch a Icelander in public.
- Do not speak rude language in public.
- Do not come late for social appointments.

22

Norway- NORGE

In General
The kingdom of Norway occupies the western part of the Scandinavian Peninsula. The country forms a narrow mountainous strip along the North Sea in the southwest and in the west the Atlantic Ocean. It has a long inland frontier with Sweden in the east, and in the northeast it borders Finland and Russia.

Oslo is the capital and largest city. The nation's outlying possessions are Svalbard and Jan Mayen in the Arctic Ocean and Bouvet and the Peter Islands in the South Atlantic; Norway also has claims in Antarctica. Because of the North Atlantic Drift, Norway has a mild and humid climate for a northern country. The country is famous for its fjords and dried fish.

A Little History
The history of Norway, before the age of the so-strongly-feared **Vikings**, is indistinct from that of the rest of Scandinavia. In the 9th century the country was still divided among numerous kings. Harold I defeated them (A.D. 900), and conquered the Shetlands and the Orkneys, but failed to establish unity. His campaigns drove many nobles to settle in Iceland and France.

Over the next two centuries, the Vikings raided widely in western Europe and established the Norse duchy of Normandy in France.

The act of union of 1814 recognized Norway as an independent kingdom, in personal union with Sweden, with its own constitution and parliament. In 1905, Norway chose to become a monarchy, and parliament elected the second son of Frederick VIII of Denmark, Haakon VII, as king of Norway.

In the late 19th and early 20th century, history shows a large-scale emigration to the United States. In that same period there were great arctic and Antarctic explorations by famous men like Nansen and Amundsen. Two outstanding cultural figures of that time were **Grieg** and **Ibsen**.
In World War I, Norway remained neutral. Norway attempted to remain neutral in World War II also, but German troops invaded and remained in Norway until the war ended in May 1945. Norway sparked international controversy in 1992 when it refused to conform to the International Whaling Treaty.

Business Profile

The country's chief industries are petroleum and natural gas production, shipping, and trading. Norwegians are direct and do not care for rituals and/or social environments when it comes to doing business.

In their corporations you find a low level of risk-taking. This makes it difficult to get a final signature on contracts, even when you have convinced their negotiator. Hard-selling techniques are not appreciated in Norway. Pressing for greater speed will probably backfire.

Although top managers make the decisions, they usually ask the opinion of project groups and lower managers. Norwegians are ready to talk business after only a few minutes of small talk. During business meetings you'll notice that Norwegians are straightforward and use moderate eye contact.

Machine Guns

Trying to get a television program sold to a very wealthy and influential **Italian** businessman in Milan, a **Norwegian** businessman went to see the "big shot" to close the deal. Upon arrival, he noticed guards with machine guns outside the gate.
Once inside and talking to the secretary, he joked about the guards and their machine guns, saying, "So, is your boss a member of the Mafia, or is he afraid of them?" He never got to see the big shot in person and was sent away with the excuse that something had come up and that he should try to make a new appointment for another time. That "other time" was never awarded.

If he only had adjusted to the culture of certain influential persons in countries such as Italy and had pretended that it was quite normal, he might have been able to close the deal.
He should have complimented the man on his security personnel, instead of making a bad joke about a phenomenon of the country that no one is really proud of having.

First Business Encounters
- Give at least one month's notice for an appointment.
- Offer a firm handshake as you make brief eye contact.
- Shake hands with everyone, coming and going.
- Tell people your first name and family name when being introduced.

Dress Code
- Dress conservatively. Men wear suit and tie; women wear suits or skirts.
- Bring formal outfits as well as casual ones.

Addressing People
- Norwegians don't insist on their titles.
- First-name basis is very common in business environments.

Business Cards
- Make sure your card is in English.
- Pay special attention to the cards they give you.

Incentives
- Expensive gifts are not appreciated. Bringing liquor is always welcome due to the high prices of luxury goods.

Doing Business
- For the first meeting you need a well-prepared agenda, and a very clear, well-structured presentation. Norwegians like to be to-the-point, even though they might take some time for small talk, the meetings will be: "strictly business."
- Emphasize facts and profitability during your presentation.
- Give an honest impression by pointing out weaknesses, and disadvantages as well as advantages.
- Trust is an important factor for them.
- When you make statements, make sure you can prove them to be true.
- Avoid boasting about your company, products, or yourself.
- Make sure that you keep your deadline/schedule promises.

Business Meals
- The person who invites you usually pays the bill.
- Norway does not have a specific business lunch culture.
- Alcoholic beverages are limited and after-work cocktails are unusual. But beware of their Aquavit the "cure of all ills".

- The Vikings used to drink from the empty skulls of their dead enemies, and the **"skaal"** toasting ritual is still an important part of their social and business gatherings. Raise your glass, look the host in the eyes, drink, lower the glass, look each other in the eyes again, and continue eating or talking.
- Upscale restaurants expect men and women to dress very well.

Table Manners and Etiquette
- All the previous written guidelines are acknowledged in Norway.

Social Events
- When walking on the street, informal dress is okay.
- Be punctual at all times, to both business and social events.
- For a social gathering, informal means nice casual clothes.
- Bring flowers, chocolates, your tax-free liquor, or a souvenir from your home country.
- Keep conversation general. Try culture, sports, art, etc., for topics.

First Business Encounters
- Never be late, not even one minute. Call them if you are late.
- Do not mention their titles.
- Do not start to bargain.

Dress Code
- Do not wear casual clothes for business appointments.
- Do not overdress by wearing flashy designer clothes and jewelry.

Addressing People
- Do not treat any person differently from another.
- Do not forget to shake hands with everyone.

Business Cards
- Do not forget to have your card in English.

Incentives
- Do not bring expensive gifts; they might consider that a bribe.

Doing Business
- Do not abruptly change the time, or place for appointments.
- Do not show emotions during negotiations.
- Do not over-promise.
- Do not interrupt a person; it is considered very rude.
- Do not change or add elements during a meeting.
- Do not try to renegotiate terms after an agreement has been made.

Business Meals
- Do not start drinking until the host or hostess has proposed a toast to the entire company.
- Do not break eye contact during the toast.
- Do not forget to inform your host upfront about special diets.
- Do not presume to seat yourself.

Table manners and Etiquette
- All the previously written guidelines still count.

Social Events
- Do not complain about the high cost of living in Norway.
- Do not talk about private topics in public.
- Do not ask personal questions and/or speak rude language in public.
- Do not come late for social appointments.
- Do not light up a cigarette in a Norwegian home without asking permission.
- Do not leave the table before your host does.

Sweden - SVERIGE

In General
The North European kingdom of Sweden (its capital is Stockholm) is part of Scandinavia. It is bordered by Norway on the west and Finland on the east. The Gulf of Bothnia and the Baltic Sea surround the east and southern part of Sweden. Sweden is known for its great nature, large pine forests with lots of moose, mountainous wilderness, and its cold climate. Also the legendary midnight sun is found in Sweden, in the north areas of Norrland.

Sweden has a large steel industry, which stretches out over the whole world. Its population is small, but as history shows, many Swedes have gained world fame. The Swedes cherish their royal family and take great pride in being part of the country that awards the world famous Nobel Prize, which was founded by industrialist Alfred Nobel in 1901.

A Little History
The infamous Vikings left their visible traces mainly on the eastern and southern parts of Europe in the 9th and 10th century. The Swedes became more and more civilized over the ages and contributed a lot to peace and unity among the Scandinavian countries.

Around A.D. 1000, after about two centuries of prosperity and power, the trade empire of the Vikings began to decline. Continental Europe began its economic rise, and the power of the Vikings in Swedish lands was taken away by the prosperous farmers of the interior plains.

In the early sixteenth century, Gustav Vasa, whose leadership established the foundations of Sweden, and Gustav II Adolf, a figure better known as the "Lion of the North," pushed Sweden into prosperity.
In 1632, after the battle of Lützen, Sweden became a troubled nation and entered a century of almost constant war.

One result of that experience has been a commitment to neutrality in subsequent European conflicts, including both World Wars. Until today, Sweden is not a member of any military alliance.

Due to this peace and neutrality, the Swedes achieved a high standard of living, aided by their modern capitalism and great social benefits.

Business Profile

Swedish businesspeople are honest, efficient, and very conscientious. They are tolerant people who believe in equality, kindness and modesty. They are very loyal toward everything they love. Their strength lies in quality; Volvo and Saab are Swedish cars that have been voted the safest cars in the world.

Swedes keep their promises; they usually deliver on time as agreed. Business managers like to have a high level of interactivity between levels of workers. They are very democratic in decision making, which sometimes can take a bit longer than you might want, so be patient. They love to work in teams and dislike displays of power and hierarchy.

Doing business with the Swedes is a pleasure; they are straightforward, love to agree on topics, and are very accommodating toward foreigners. Swedes treat their business opponents with a lot of respect and expect the same behavior from them. Here is what you should and shouldn't do in order to smooth the path toward doing business successfully.

Silverware Versus Chopsticks

In one of the bigger **Swedish** steel factories, a businessman from **Japan** was taken out to dinner. Being more comfortable with chopsticks than regular silverware, the man dropped his silverware by accident and wondered what to do next. Do I pick it up, wipe it clean, and continue using it, or ask for clean silverware, or maybe even ask for chopsticks?

In a case like this, there is really nothing to worry about. Everybody drops silverware once in a while. The etiquette, however, tells you to ask for clean silverware. Don't even bother to pick it up, unless it is easy enough. Concentrate on your business dinner and don't attract attention to small mistakes such as these. Regarding chopsticks, you will not find them in regular restaurants in Europe unless you go to an Asian restaurant, e.g., Chinese or Japanese.

First Business Encounters
- Make appointments a minimum of two weeks in advance.
- Shake hands with everyone when you are being introduced and when you are leaving.
- Tell people your family name upon introduction.
- Look people briefly in the eyes.

Dress Code
- Prepare for cold weather.
- Bring lots of formal outfits.
- Men should wear suit and tie and women suits or skirts.

Addressing People
- First-name basis is normal for Swedes.
- Titles are not important in Sweden.

Business Cards
- Bring enough cards; Swedes like them.
- Make sure your card is in English.

Incentives
- Liquor makes a much-appreciated gift; it is very expensive in Sweden.
- You may give presents when closing a business transaction.

Doing Business
- For the first meeting you need a well-prepared detailed agenda.
- Be patient with Swedes; they need a few meetings to get used to you.

Business Meals
- Usually the person who invites you pays the bill.
- Upscale restaurants expect men and women to dress well.
- Partners, or spouses may join you for a business dinner but not for business lunches.
- Cocktail hour in Sweden will provide you with their Aquavit, which is a very strong clear liquor. Try to finish it in one sip.
- The smorgasbord is a famous Swedish way of eating. You have to make several trips to the table and taste the variety of food.
- When you are the guest of honor, you may thank your host by saying, "*Tack for maten*" [Thank you for the food].

Table Manners and Etiquette
- All the previous written guidelines are acknowledged in Sweden.

Social Events

- When walking on the street, informal dress is okay.
- Be punctual at all times, to both business and social events.
- For a social gathering, informal means nice casual clothes.
- You may sunbathe in the nude when you are at the beach.
- Keep conversation general; try nature, literature, art, etc., for topics.
- Gifts are expected for social events. If you bring flowers, be sure to unwrap them before handing them to the hostess.
- Make sure the flowers come in odd numbers (an old tradition).
- More-precious gifts are expected when you are staying at a family's house.

First Business Encounters
- Never be late, not even one minute.
- Do not be impatient during meetings; Swedes like to discuss a lot.
- Do not push issues.

Dress Code
- Do not wear casual clothes for business appointments.
- Do not overdress by wearing flashy designer clothes.

Addressing People
- Do not insist on your title.
- Do not digress or use a lot of superlatives.

Business Cards
- Do not forget to have your card in English.

Incentives
- Do not bring a present for the first encounter.

Doing Business
- Do not abruptly change the time and place for appointments.
- Do not show emotions during negotiations.

Business Meals
- Do not take your aperitif to the table. Finish it before dinner is served.
- Do not start drinking until the host or hostess has said "skol" [cheers].
- Do not take the last serving on a platter. This is considered rude.

Table Manners and Etiquette
- All the previously written guidelines still count.

Social Events
- Do not show emotions in public.
- Do not talk about private topics in public or ask personal questions.
- Do not backslap, hug or kiss, or touch a Swede in public.
- Do not speak rude language in public.
- It is not appropriate to be "fashionably late" for social appointments.
- Do not give your host anything that is easily obtainable in Sweden.
- Do not bring chrysanthemums or white lilies; those are used for funerals.
- Do not bring red roses or orchids, as those indicate romance, unless you have romantic feelings for your host, of course.
- Do not stare at naked bodies if you see people sunbathing in the nude.

Business Presentations

Preparing for his trip to **Europe**, a **Chinese** businessman did some heavy research on the Internet to become familiar with the ways of his European counterparts. Knowing that he had to have a very well-structured presentation, he prepared about 30 pages in Power Point. Upon arrival he showed his impressive presentation, that consisted mainly of text. He noticed, that after slide number 10, people started to lose interest.

He struggled through the rest of his "show" and waited for questions, which did not emerge. Coming from a culture, where asking questions really is not done, he did not think much of it, until one of the participants asked him, if he had his presentation on paper as well. He did not!

Graphics are imperative for a good understanding of your presentation. In general, people learn and understand things using two different ways, either by
- **listening, hearing, and reading (the auditive ones), or**
- **watching, looking, and picturing things (the visual ones).**

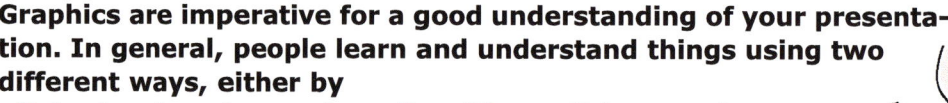

You find the visual ones mostly in technical professions and the auditive ones more in administrative or sales jobs.
You have to accommodate both "types", because you will not know beforehand what type of person will be attending your presentation. Therefore, it is important to illustrate your story with images, pictures, drawings, etc.

TIP
- **A presentation should contain no more pages or slides per minute than you are speaking. If your presentation takes 30 minutes, try to keep your slides/pages under 30.**
- **The pages you show, must only have the keywords or figures of your story and also some images, pictures, and graphics or such.**
- **Have your whole presentation on paper as well.**
- **Bring at least as many copies as there will be participants in the meeting, in order for people to be able to read everything over, after you finished.**

Finland - SUOMI

In General
The Republic of Finland, (Helsinki is its capital) borders the Gulf of Bothnia and Sweden in the west, Norway in the north, Russia in the east, and the Gulf of Finland and the Baltic Sea in the south. This Nordic country includes the Åland Islands in the Gulf of Bothnia. Beautiful forested Finland is also called the land of a thousand lakes; however, there are at least 60,000 lakes to be found.

The main factor influencing Finland's climate is the country's geographical position, which shows characteristics of both a maritime and a continental climate, including severe cold in winter and extreme heat in the short summer. During the months of the midnight sun, the coastal area is a sailing and fishing paradise. Inland, the largest untouched wilderness in Europe attracts thousands of nature lovers.

Finland's top designer, Alvar Aalto, embellished the world with his building and furniture design; the composer Jean Sibelius inspired many music lovers worldwide. Finns are, for the most, quiet and a bit shy. All they need to be happy is: a cottage by a lake and a properly stoked sauna.

A Little History
The first Finnish-speaking persons that entered the region were mostly nomadic hunters and fishers who migrated into Finland from the south. By the 8th century they had displaced the small number of Lapps, who lived in central and South Finland and who were forced to move to the far north of the country, where they still live today. In the 13th century, Sweden conquered the country. Finland suffered severely in the recurring wars between Sweden and Russia.
During the Napoleonic Wars, Finland was conquered by Russia and annexed in 1809. Following the Bolshevik success in the Russian Revolution (1917), the parliament proclaimed the independence of Finland. After a civil war and several government crises during the 1930s, Finland followed a neutralist foreign policy, and in 1932 it signed a non-aggression treaty with the USSR. However, in late November 1939, shortly after the start of World War II, Finland was invaded by Soviet troops again.
In the postwar period, Social Democrats and the Agrarian Union dominated politics.

In 1955 Finland joined the United Nations. In 1994, Martti Ahtisaari, a Social Democrat and diplomat, became Finland's first president elected by direct popular vote.

Business Profile

Seniority is held in high esteem in the conservative business branches. In this egalitarian business culture, senior managers treat their subordinates with respect. Even junior managers often have considerable independent decision-making authority. This informality facilitates the exchange of ideas within Finnish companies. More and more, younger people of both sexes hold executive positions today and the number of women in managerial positions is quite high.

Women and men are treated as equals in the work place. Business meetings and negotiations are to-the-point, and usually begin on time with rather little small talk. Negotiations are mainly held in offices, not restaurants. Finns are well prepared for negotiations and presentations.

They prefer modesty without sacrificing credibility, and hearing technical details rather than sales talk. In fact, they are not very talkative at all and prefer silences during conversation. They have a dry, understated, and ironic sense of humor. They value modesty, honesty, reliability, and cleanliness.

Knees and Shoes

You can't help it when you are really tall and thus have problems with most of the seats you are offered.
Somehow you have to find a way of placing your legs in order to be comfortable and yet inoffensive. Here is what happened to a tall **Finn** in **England**. During a negotiation, the Norwegian crossed one leg over the other, trying to push his knee down a bit, while sitting behind a desk. However, the sole of his shoe pointed toward a lady that was sitting next to him. She turned her back to him and refused to address him. Why?

It is an absolute no-no to show the sole of your shoe to anyone, as it is perceived as an insult. Instead he should have put both his feet firmly on the floor without crossing his legs. Apart from that, it is also not done to have one knee sticking out, above the desk or table where you are sitting. The only extremities that are allowed above or on the table, are the arms and hands.

First Business Encounters
- Give at least one or two weeks' notice for an appointment made by telephone; allow at least a month for an appointment made by mail.
- Prior appointments are necessary and preferably are made by phone.
- Note that Finnish telephone etiquette requires giving your full name, when both calling and answering the phone.
- Business introductions consist of exchanging cards, names etc.
- Offer a firm handshake as you make brief eye contact.
- Shake hands with everyone, both coming and going.
- Tell people your first name and family name when being introduced.
- Finns like to hear about your trip upon arrival.
- They take pride in their architecture, technology, and art, so you might want to say something nice about it.

Dress Code
- Check the weather report of the country; it can be very cold.
- Bring formal outfits as well as casual ones. Men wear dark suits and ties, women wear fashionable suits or skirts.

Addressing People
- Finns like their titles, and they do take pride in them.
- It is advisable to address businesspeople by their titles when first introduced, but it is not necessary after that.
- Safe small-talk topics are weather, culture, history and travel.

Business Cards
- Bring enough cards; Finns like them.
- Make sure your card is in English and provides your title(s) and position, for Finns have a great respect for academic education.
- Pay special attention to the cards they give you; it will show how you will treat your business counterpart.

Incentives
- You may bring something from your country as a token of appreciation to your business counterpart or host.

Doing Business
- Send an agenda before the meeting, as well as your biography.
- For the first meeting, you need a well-prepared agenda, and a very clear, well-structured presentation. Finns like to be to-the-point; even though they might take some time for small talk, the meetings will be "strictly business."
- Set clear goals, in both meetings and work strategy, and encourage your Finnish counterparts to work independently.

- Finns are very straightforward and direct, and not only in the business environment.
- Finns do keep their promises and expect the same from you.
- When you make statements, make sure you can prove them to be true. Finns like to see facts.
- Be prepared to work independently and show self-discipline in your work.
- Avoid boasting about your company, products or yourself, Finns are not impressed by superlatives.

Business Meals

- Dinner is an excellent opportunity for business discussions.
- Visitors are normally taken to restaurants or company lodges.
- There is no strict dress code, but a jacket and tie are recommended for business-class restaurants.
- The trend is toward milder alcohol drinks and less volume.
- Their law prohibits smoking in offices and public places.
- Upscale restaurants expect men and women to dress very well.

Table Manners and Etiquette

- All the previous written guidelines are strictly observed in Finland.
- Only bread and shrimp are eaten by hand.
- When passing the pepper or salt shaker, put it on the table in front of the person.

Social Events
- When walking on the street, informal dress is okay.
- Be punctual at all times, to both business and social events.
- For a social gathering, informal means nice casual clothes.
- Remove your outdoor shoes when entering a home.
- Keep conversation general. Try culture, sports, art etc. for topics.
- Gifts are acceptable for social events: flowers or good chocolate.
- More-precious gifts are appreciated when you are staying at a family's house.

- Finns often invite their guests to the sauna (men and women go separately), and it is polite to accept the invitation, but it is not a must.
- Finish the food on your plate; Finns don't appreciate waste.
- Keep your jacket on during dinner, unless you are told otherwise.
- Offer to help clean up after dinner.
- Thank the host(ess) before you say goodbye to other guests when you are leaving.

First Business Encounters
• Never be late, not even one minute.
• Do not forget to mention their titles.
• Do not engage in small talk.
• Do not forget to mention your first and last name.

Dress Code
• Do not wear casual clothes for business appointments.
• Do not overdress by wearing flashy designer clothes and jewelry.

Addressing People
• Do not treat any person differently from another.
• Do not forget to shake hands with everyone, coming and going.
• Do not (ever) interrupt someone.

Business Cards
• Do not forget to have your card in English.

Incentives
• Do not bring a gift for the first encounter.

Doing Business
• Do not abruptly change the time and place for appointments.
• Do not show emotions during negotiations.

Business Meals
• Do not take your aperitif to the table. Finish it before dinner is served.
• Do not start drinking until the host or hostess has proposed a toast to the entire company.
• Do not break eye contact during the toast.
• Do not forget to inform your host upfront about special diets. Finns like their reindeer stew which can be heavy on the stomach.
• Do not presume to seat yourself.
• Do not start eating before your host does.

Table Manners and Etiquette
• All the previously written guidelines still count.

Social Events
- Do not talk about private topics in public.
- Do not speak about very personal matters.
- Do not ask direct questions about salaries, taxes, and religion.
- Do not praise the Swedes to your Finnish counterparts.
- Do not backslap, hug or kiss, or touch a Finn in public.
- Do not ask personal questions.
- Do not speak rude language in public.
- Do not come late for social appointments.
- Do not forget to take your shoes off.
- Do not bring flowers in even numbers.
- Do not bring yellow or white flowers (funeral only).
- Do not talk business in someone's house.
- Do not seat yourself.
- Do not start eating before your host does.

Denmark - DANMARK

In General
This small country in the Nordic area of Europe, with Copenhagen for its capital, is located in between the North Sea and the Baltic Sea. Denmark also includes the Faeroe Islands and Greenland in the North Atlantic. The bulk of Denmark is the peninsula Jutland, which has a border with Germany of just 68 kilometer.

The rest of the country consists of 406 islands, 78 of which are inhabited. The highest point measures 170 meters above sea level. No one in Denmark is more than 50 kilometer from the sea. The climate is a temperate coastal climate, which causes a lot of rain and plenty of wind.

Danes have a tendency to take the ups and downs of life with a touch of irony. The tone between Danes is relaxed. With an open economy and great dependence on what is happening in the surrounding world, the Danes have benefited from their international attitude.

Denmark made (and makes) a lot of children from all over the world very happy. Who has never heard a fairy tale written by Hans Christian Andersen? And who has never played with the colorful LEGO blocks?

A Little History
The origin of Denmark is uncertain, but up into the 11th century the Danes were known as Vikings, who colonized, raided, and traded in much of Europe. At various times Denmark has ruled England, Norway, Sweden, Finland, Iceland, Ireland, and parts of the Virgin Islands; Tranquebar in India; parts of the Baltic coast and what is now, northern Germany.

After the European revolutions, Denmark became a constitutional monarchy in 1849. In 1864 Denmark was forced to cede Schleswig-Holstein to Prussia in a bad defeat from which their national identity still suffers. After that, Denmark held a policy of neutrality, and stayed neutral during World War I. On April 9, 1940, Denmark was invaded by Nazi Germany. After the war, Denmark became a member of NATO, and in 1973, the European Union.

Business Profile
Danish businesspeople are pragmatic, modest, tolerant, and show international orientation. They are easy-going, flexible and patient in negotiations, and are good listeners.

In their businesses there is no clear hierarchical structure, and leadership is by achievement. They approach people the informal way. They also like a low-key approach, which is often marked by humor. Danes are very punctual; they don't like hierarchy and will not respect it in their business dealings. They are known for their ability to secure good deals without making enemies. Denmark is very progressive when it comes to equality between men and women. Businesswomen travelers will find it highly pleasing to engage in business in Denmark. It is possible for them to initiate meetings and also social engagements with men.

Cell Phones

In JFK Airport in **New York**, many people were waiting to leave for **Copenhagen (Denmark)** from the international concourse. One man had been on his cell phone for 15 minutes, talking loudly as if he was hard of hearing. Unaware (or not caring) of the nuisance he was causing the other passengers, he kept talking and talking. Already some people frowned at him, especially a rather neatly dressed older man. Everybody could follow his conversation, which included some interesting business details. When boarding started, the man was still on his phone and continued even in the plane. Before take-off he had to shut down his phone. His neatly dressed neighbor turned to him and said, "So, you are Mister Johnson, with whom I have a meeting tomorrow in my office at 12:00. I am really glad you already gave me so much important information."

No comment on this one, but here's some well-meaning advice. You never know who is listening in on your conversations. So, if you suddenly turn deaf when using a cell phone, you might consider purchasing a hearing aid.

First Business Encounters
- Make appointments a minimum of two weeks in advance.
- Danish business introductions consist of a formal and solemn exchange.
- Be sure to stand up before extending your hand.
  Offer a firm handshake as you make eye contact.
- Shake hands with everyone, coming and going.
- Tell people your first name and family name when being introduced.
- Do show appreciation for their hospitality; business events include social activities.

Dress Code
- Prepare for cold and rainy weather.
- Bring formal outfits as well as casual ones. Men wear suits and white shirts and simple ties. Women wear stylish suits or skirts.

Addressing People
- First-name basis is normal after having established an understanding.
- Titles are not all that important in Denmark.

Business Cards
- Bring enough cards. Danes like them. Make sure your card is in English.
- If the company you represent was founded ten or more years ago, be sure to list that information on your business card. Stability is an important characteristic to the Danes.

Incentives
- Liquor makes a much-appreciated gift, because it is expensive in Denmark.
- You may bring gifts, but they are not required in a business relationship.

Doing Business
- For the first meeting you need a well-prepared agenda.
- Danes seem unfriendly and uncaring, but in social settings they are nice.

Business Meals
- Usually the person who invites you pays the bill.
- Upscale restaurants expect men and women to dress well.
- The food might appear strange to you, so take small portions to start.
- Wait until the host has proposed a toast before you start eating.
  A toast is: "*skal!*"

Table Manners and Etiquette
- All the previous written guidelines are acknowledged in Denmark.

Social Events

- When walking on the street, informal dress is okay; such as jeans and sneakers, but they should be clean and look nice.
- Be punctual at all times, to both business and social events.
- For a social gathering, informal means nice casual clothes.
- Keep conversation general; try: culture, sports, art, etc., for topics.
- Gifts are expected for social events. If you bring flowers, don't bring white ones.
- More-precious gifts are appreciated when you are staying at a family's house.

First Business Encounters
- Never be late, not even one minute.
- Do not push issues.

Dress Code
- Do not wear casual clothes for business appointments.
- Do not overdress by wearing flashy designer clothes.

Addressing People
- Do not insist on your title.
- Do not digress or use a lot of superlatives.

Business Cards
- Do not forget to have your card in English.

Incentives
- Do not bring a gift for the first encounter.

Doing Business
- Do not abruptly change the time and place for appointments.
- Do not show emotions during negotiations.

Business Meals
- Do not take your aperitif to the table. Finish it before dinner is served.
- Do not start drinking until the host or hostess has proposed a toast.
- Do not break eye contact during the toast.
- Don't refuse when the Danes offer you their traditional very potent drink "Aquavit," which means: "water of life." Expect some "heat," though.
- Do not take the last serving on a platter.

Table Manners and Etiquette
- All the previously written guidelines still count.

Social Events
- Do not talk about private topics in public.
- Do not use sexist or racist humor.
- Do not backslap, hug or kiss, or touch a Dane in public.
- Do not ask personal questions.
- Do not speak rude language in public.
- Do not come "fashionably late" for social appointments.
- Do not leave food untouched on your plate; you will offend the host.
- Do not leave the table before your host does.
- Do not leave right away after dinner.
- Do not be shocked if you see women sunbathing topless.
- Do not stare at the topless bodies of women, no matter how tempting it may be.

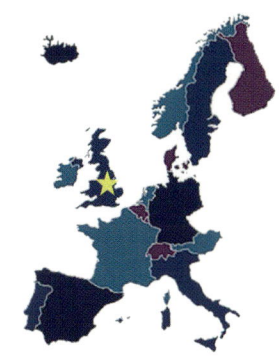

United Kingdom - GREAT BRITAIN

In General
Europe's biggest island is officially called: the United Kingdom of Great Britain and Northern Ireland. The UK consists of three distinct entities: England, Scotland, and Wales. Its capital is London. The UK is situated between the North Atlantic, and the North Sea, northwest of France and opposite Belgium and the Netherlands. Surrounded by water, its climate is a maritime one, therefore, England has to endure a lot of rain. A real British gentleman never leaves his home without his umbrella. The country gets a variety of weather, yet the rain will always be waiting around the corner. The UK has produced quite a few celebrities, world-famous writers such as Sir Walter Scott and William Shakespeare, and world-renowned musicians such as the Beatles. Not only persons have become famous; the Rolls-Royce and Bentley are prestigious cars that can be found in many royal households worldwide.

A Little History
England has existed as a unified kingdom since the 10th century, when supposedly witches, druids, ghosts, and other fairy-tale figures, helped to create some chaos every now and then. The union with Wales was enacted in 1284; the Act of Union of 1707 led to Scotland joining England and Wales as Great Britain.

It is said that knight-hood originates in the UK. King Arthur and the Knights of the Round Table are more than just storybook figures. The British Empire stretched over one-fourth of the earth's surface due to the brave sailors, who sailed the world seas and conquered quite a few pieces of land, such as Australia, New Zealand, lots of isles in the Caribbean and isles along the coast of South America. They traded a part of the USA with the Dutch, which caused the USA to become an English-speaking nation. Moreover, English became a global language. The kingdom, however, saw many turbulent years pass before it became the nation it is today.

The first half of the 20th century saw the UK's strength seriously depleted in two World Wars. The second half witnessed the dismantling of the empire and the UK rebuilding itself into a modern and prosperous European nation.
From time to time its royal family stirs up emotions around the world, and so does Harry Potter.

Business Profile
British businesspeople are very polite, humorous, and love courtesy. They are also traditional, stubborn, patriotic and sometimes a bit eccentric.

They love understated and subtle humor, which really can dominate their interactions with foreigners. They suffer from a severe bureaucracy. British organizations have varying degrees of hierarchy, ranging from a rather flat and consensus style of management to a steep, hierarchical, top-down structure.

A wide range of input is valued and a consensus may be reached, but the final decision still rests with the most powerful individual. They love "fair play" and hate the feeling of being "taken." Somehow, it seems that they will always have an ace up their sleeves, which they throw out at the least- expected moment. Reason and lots of polite smiles will help you find out about those aces. Brits don't make decisions fast and seem a bit vague, so listen carefully to what they are saying, because they have the advantage of the language.

First Business Encounters
- Do arrive at business encounters with a good supply of jokes and anecdotes.
- Make appointments at least two weeks in advance and confirm them upon arrival.
- Try to display logic and common sense.
- Punctuality is appreciated but it's okay when you arrive a little later (as much as 15 minutes).
- Introductions consist of introducing one another, and a little social talk.
- Offer a firm handshake as you make brief eye contact.
- Keep a wide distance between yourself and the participant during conversation.
- Shake hands with everyone upon arriving and leaving.
- Tell people your first name and family name when being introduced.

Dress Code
- Check the weather report of the county; it can be cold and rainy.
- Bring formal outfits as well as casual ones, and of course an umbrella.
- Conservative dress is the norm for men and women. Darker colors predominate, such as black, dark blue, charcoal grey and heavier fabrics.

Addressing People
- Brits don't insist on their titles, but they do take pride in them.
- First-name basis is very common in business environments.
- You should always wait to be invited to use first names.
- Try to follow protocol, especially when dealing with older members of the "establishment."

Business Cards
- Bring a plentiful supply of cards.
- Make sure your card is in English and provides your title(s) and position.
- Business cards are normally exchanged at the end of a meeting.

Incentives
- Giving gifts is not a normal part of British business culture.
- At the conclusion of a deal, it might be appropriate to give a commemorative item with an inscription to mark the occasion.

Doing Business
- For the first meeting, you need a well-prepared agenda.
- Make sure you have the proper materials for effective presentations.

- Meetings may appear rather anarchic with little apparent structure.
- During initial meetings, facial expressions are kept to a minimum. Brits like to play at "being-absent-minded," however, this is a trick they use to throw you off balance.
- Remain observant and professional even when a meeting seems to be informal.
- Give them the necessary time to make a full assessment of you as an individual as well as of your proposal and your company.
- The decision maker may be the quietest person around the table.
- Decision-making can be a slow process. Don't pressure the key figure.
- Brits do keep their promises and expect the same from you.
- When you make statements, make sure you can prove them to be true.
- Avoid boasting about your company, products or yourself.
- The British respect qualities such as honesty and straightforwardness.

Business Meals

- British cuisine is not what most people prefer. Make sure you understand the contents of the dishes before you order them.
- The best time for a serious and productive business meal is lunch.
- Breakfast meetings are not popular (even in London).
- Dinner tends to be reserved for more sociable entertaining where spouses are welcome as well and talking business is mostly off the menu.
- Lunch is generally taken between noon and 2:00 p.m. in restaurants.
- The famous "high tea," by the way, is between 4:00 p.m. and 6:00 p.m.; it consists of a hot dish, sandwiches, scones, and cakes.
- Upscale restaurants expect men and women to dress very well.
- Be sure to follow the protocol your host is showing.

Table Manners and Etiquette
- All the previous written guidelines are strictly observed in the UK.

Social Events

- When walking on the street, informal dress is okay.
- One should not arrive too promptly for social events; try to arrive fifteen minutes after the specified time.
- For a social gathering, informal means: nice casual clothes.
- British businesspeople like to socialize in a local pub with their colleagues after work.
- Beer is the most popular drink on informal occasions. When ordering beer, women traditionally order half-pints and men pints. The macho British drinking culture frowns on men drinking halves.
- Keep conversation general. Try culture, sports, soccer, etc., for topics.
- Gifts are appreciated for social events. You can bring flowers, but not roses.

First Business Encounters
- Do not appear to be overly serious.
- Do not forget to bring jokes.
- Do not breathe in someone's face or on someone's neck.
- Do not stare too long at people.
- Do not (ever) talk while your hands are in your pockets; they might think you have something to hide or otherwise.

Dress Code
- Do not wear casual clothes for business appointments.
- Do not overdress by wearing flashy designer clothes and jewelry.

Addressing People
- Do not treat any person differently from another.
- Do not forget to shake hands with everyone.

Business Cards
- Do not give your card right away.

Incentives
- Do not bring a gift for the first encounter.

Doing Business
- Do not abruptly change the time and place for appointments.
- Do not show emotions during negotiations.
- Do not feel intimidated by their "playing absent minded"; it is part of their show.

Business Meals
- Do not take your aperitif to the table. Finish it before food is served.
- Do not start drinking until the host or hostess has proposed a toast to the entire company. A common toast is, "*cheers!*"
- Do not break eye contact during the toast.
- Do not forget to inform your host upfront about special diets.
- Do not presume to seat yourself.

Table Manners and Etiquette
- All the previously written guidelines still count.

United kingdom

Social Events
- Do not talk about private topics in public.
- Do not backslap, hug or kiss, or touch a Brit in public.
- Do not ask personal questions.
- Do not speak rude language in public.
- Do not cut into waiting lines.
- Do not invade someone's private space.
- Do not raise your voice at any time.

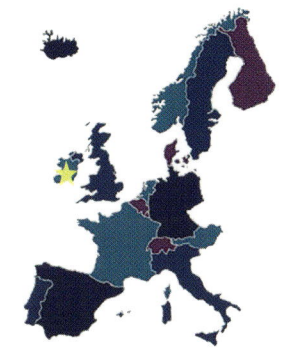

Ireland - EIRE

In General
Situated on the northwest side of the UK, the Republic of Ireland (the capital is Dublin) is surrounded by water, which makes it an island. The Gulf Stream exercises a benign influence, giving the island a temperate climate. The rain is legendary in Ireland. It rains roughly twice as much in the west of the country than in the east. World-famous Guinness beer comes from the emerald isle of wondrous hilly green countryside, where you are likely to encounter (as some people whisper) leprechauns, fairies, and the little people. Their beautiful and intriguing folksongs and dances have traveled all over the world and make people wonder whether the fairy tales are maybe true.

A Little History
The first settlers arrived between 8000 and 7000 B.C.; these were followed by the first Celtic-speaking people between 700 and 500 B.C. and Viking settlers in the 9th century A.D. English involvement in Ireland began with the arrival of the Normans in the 10th century, but England did not have full control until the whole island was conquered in 1653. Prior to 1801, Ireland enjoyed a self-governing status under the parliament of Ireland. In 1801 this parliament was abolished and Ireland became an integral part of a new United Kingdom.

In 1922 six counties of Ireland seceded from the United Kingdom and became the independent state known today as the Republic of Ireland. The remainder of the island, known as Northern Ireland, remained part of the UK. The republic suffered for decades afterwards, but since the 1990s economic success has come back. Nothing good happened for Northern Ireland; since its establishment it has been dominated by ongoing conflicts between Catholics and Protestants.

Business Profile
Irish businesspeople are very charming, friendly and open minded. They show great respect for their church, family, and country; not necessarily in this order, though. Many businesses are family owned and family run. Promotion is often given to family members first above other employees, regardless of skills and experiences, so check who's related to whom when you meet them and be careful of sisters, cousins, and third cousins; they might pop out of the woodwork when you least expect them!

The Irish love to tell stories and like to exaggerate a bit, but that happens usually when their minds are under the influence of Guinness beer, which you will probably experience as well, when you are their guest. They have a hierarchical society that shows respect and obedience toward managers and leaders.

The subordinates display little initiative and must be encouraged to participate fully in business dealings. The Irish like to display a love of poetry and passion in their communication; therefore, meetings can become chaotic and confusing. They do not show great respect for agendas or schedules, but welcome enthusiasm and creativity. Their feedback can often be ambiguous, or even appear to be devious, maybe because a little leprechaun might be hiding inside every Irish mind.

Everything is Bigger

Most Americans are proud of their country, but some of them boast about it in an annoying way. An **American** businessman in **Ireland** was entertained and taken for a tour. Everything he was shown, he commented on with the words, "Nice, but it is bigger in the USA." At a certain point the Irish host got a bit tired of his attitude and thought of something to use to get back at him. They came across a beautiful lake and the American asked him what that was. The Irishman replied, "Oh that; that is some water from the leaking radiator of my car."

Of course, this is a rather silly joke, but it illustrates how boasting can be perceived. So please, do keep a low profile and try to compliment the inhabitants on their country, because they are just as proud of theirs as you are of yours.

First Business Encounters
- Arrange an appointment about two weeks in advance.
- Try to be punctual; when you are a few minutes late for a meeting, it will be overlooked.
- When they are late, you just have to be patient.
- Irish business introductions consist of exchanging cards, names etc., and a lot of small talk.
- Offer a firm handshake as you make brief eye contact.
- Shake hands with everyone, coming and going.
- When speaking to an Irish person, keep an arm's length from the person.
- Don't break eye contact with an Irish person when he or she is talking to you.
- Tell people your first name and family name when being introduced.
- The Irish like to hear about your trip upon arrival.

Dress Code
- Check the weather report; it can be cold and rainy; bring an umbrella.
- Bring formal outfits as well as casual ones. Men wear suits and ties, women wear fashionable suits or skirts.
- Casual attire is allowed in many corporations.

Addressing People
- The Irish don't insist on their titles.
- First-name basis is very common in business environments.
- Silence is seen as rudeness, and it makes you appear cold and unfriendly.
- Speak plainly and expect what you say to be taken literally. In turn, interpret what the Irish say to you in the same direct manner.

Business Cards
- Bring enough cards. The Irish like them.
- Make sure your card is in English; professional or academic titles do not necessarily command respect.
- Professional titles are not prominent in Irish business culture, and are usually dismissed as pretentious.
- Pay attention to the cards they give you, so you know who is who.

Incentives
- Generally, gift giving is not part of Irish business culture. But if you are invited to a home for dinner, it's okay to bring flowers, chocolates, or even better, a book, or craft from your home country.

Doing Business
- It is customary to shake hands at the beginning and end of a meeting.
- Avoid boasting about your company, products, or yourself; the Irish are not impressed by superlatives.
- Keep your presentation simple and to-the-point, since digressions or excessive details will not be well-received by an Irish audience. Irish businesspeople are usually in a hurry, so meetings will be, "strictly business".
- For the first meeting you need a well-prepared agenda, and a very clear, well-structured presentation.
- Be aware of giving away too much too early; your ideas may get stolen from you. Irish in the private sector are always hungry for new ideas and they do steal with pride.
- Decision making will be fast, once you've got to the top man or woman. Unless you get to the right person, it will not happen.
- Don't expect wild promises to come true!

Business Meals

- Lunch and dinner are excellent opportunities for business discussions.
- The Irish like to drink, so know that you are in for some pub hours.
- In the pub, you are expected to pay for a round of drinks.
- When hosting a dinner or lunch at a restaurant, it is fairly customary to drink wine, but Guinness or tea may be preferred.
- At lunchtime, most people will not take a drink.
- The Irish are extremely hospitable and often pick up the tab; however, don't assume they always do so.

Table Manners and Etiquette
- All the previous written guidelines are acknowledged in Ireland.

Social Events
- Walking on the street, informal dress is okay.
- Be punctual at all times, to both business and social events.
- For a social gathering, informal means nice casual clothes.
- Maintaining personal space is important in this culture.
- The Irish find arguments and opinionated conversation entertaining, so don't hesitate to express your views if they are sincere.
- Expect some heavy drinking during entertainment.
- Gifts are acceptable for social events.
- More-precious gifts are appreciated when you are staying at a family's house.

First Business Encounters
- Never be late. If you have to be late, make sure you call to tell them.
- Do not forget to shake hands with everybody.
- Do not stand to close to a person.
- Do not boast about your titles.
- Do not compare Ireland with England, and be careful not to praise the British.

Dress Code
- Do not wear casual clothes for business appointments.
- Do not overdress by wearing flashy designer clothes and jewelry.

Addressing People
- Do not treat any person differently from another.
- Do not forget to shake hands with everyone.
- Do not use sarcasm or act in any way snobbish or superior.

Business Cards
- Do not forget to have your card in English.
- Do not "advertise" your title. Announcing your title when meeting an Irish person may be perceived as a form of boasting.

Incentives
- Do not bring a gift for the first encounter.

Doing Business
- Do not abruptly change the time and place for appointments.
- Do not show emotions during negotiations.
- Do not trust them at first sight; they all have a bit of leprechaun in them.

Business Meals
- Do not forget to give a round of drinks in the pub.
- Do not start drinking until the host or hostess has proposed a toast to the entire company.
- Do not break eye contact during the toast.

Table Manners and Etiquette
- All the previously written guidelines still count.

Social Events

- Do not talk about topics that are currently controversial in Ireland including, the Catholic Church, the English, and immigrants.
- Do not backslap, hug or kiss, or touch an Irish person in public.
- Do not ask personal questions.
- Do not speak rude language in public.
- Do not come late for social appointments.
- Do not leave large amounts of food on your plate; you will offend the host.
- Do not leave the table before your host does.
- Do not leave right away after dinner.

The Netherlands - NEDERLAND

In General
The north European kingdom the Netherlands, also known as Holland, is part of the Benelux (Belgium, Netherlands, and Luxemburg). Its capital is Amsterdam. The Netherlands are bordered by the North Sea in the west, Germany in the east and Belgium in the south. This small country is known, among other things, for its tulips, windmills, and delightful cheese. Great painters originated from this small country. To this day the paintings of Van Gogh and Rembrandt are worth millions and millions of dollars, or as the Dutch would say, "euros." The country holds a temperate maritime climate, but most of the time you will find it overcast, cold, and raining. The best time to visit will be around April and May; the weather will be a bit nicer and all the flower fields will cover most of the country.

A Little History
The Netherlands date from the 1st century B.C., under Roman rule. By 800 the territory was ruled by Charlemagne, a Frankish king. The Netherlands passed from the control of the dukes of Bourgogne during the early 16th century into the hands of the Habsburg emperor Charles V. He in turn granted control of the Netherlands to his son, Philip II, who led the Lowlands into an 80-year war from 1568 to 1648.

During this war the seven main provinces united, and thus the Netherlands was created. The main province then was South Holland; therefore, the country is still known as **Holland**. By the mid-17th century, the country was a big commercial and maritime power. It took control over Indonesia, New Guinea, Suriname, South Africa, New York, and some islands in the Caribbean. However, all over the world you will find footprints of the Dutch due to their sailing adventures and discoveries. During both World Wars the nation suffered hardship through loss of trade and heavy destruction by Nazi Germany. The following years they tried to rebuild the country and to restore trade and industry. Indonesia was given back to its people in 1949. New Guinea gained its independence in 1962 and Suriname in 1975. Although they are very easy-going and open minded, they are also very proud of being Dutch. Their Heineken beer is famous and so is the royal Dutch Shell. Maybe that is why they think that:

"You ain't much, when you ain't Dutch."

Business Profile

The Dutch are known to be honest, hard-working, very ambitious, and efficient businesspeople. They are also very tolerant, and have a great sense for international cultures, but like to behave the "proper way."

Managers depend on their subordinates to help in the decision-making process. They don't like emotional arguments or hard-sell tactics and don't appreciate sarcastic humor. Open discussion is welcome, but confrontation is not acceptable. The Dutch like to win during negotiations. Contracts are considered to be "written in stone," and penalty clauses play an important role.

Royal Respect

A long, long time ago in the kingdom of **the Netherlands**, the ruling queen Wilhelmina organized an official dinner for a visiting representative from an **African** country. Once seated, the visitor mistook the fingerbowl for a drinking bowl and took a sip of the lemon water. The waiters, waitresses, and members of the court, who were present started to laugh.

The queen, however, took her finger bowl as well, raising it elegantly while proposing a toast in honor of the visiting guest. She then took a sip and all the dinner guests had to copy her. By doing this, the queen prevented embarrassment for her visitor. That was her way of showing **utmost respect** for the guest who obviously didn't know how to handle his tableware.

First Business Encounters
- Give at least one or two weeks' notice for an appointment made by telephone; allow at least a month for an appointment made by mail.
- Dutch business introductions consist of exchanging cards, names, etc., and offering you something to drink. Coffee and tea time are very important in the Lowlands, and you will find them often scheduled in many companies.
- Offer a firm handshake as you make eye contact; Dutch people like to look you straight in the eye to find out what type of person you are. If you look away, they think you are sneaky; if you look straight back at them, they like you.
- Coming and going, you have to shake hands firmly; Dutch don't like to shake hands with a "wet newspaper," as they call the feeling of shaking hands in a "sissy way."
- Tell people your first name and family name when being introduced.
- The Dutch like to hear about your trip upon arrival; tell them how it went.
- They take pride in their offices, so you might want to say something nice about it.

Dress Code
- Check the weather report of the country, it can be cold and rainy.
- Bring formal outfits as well as casual ones. Men wear suit and tie; women wear fashionable outfits.
- Casual attire is allowed in many corporations. The Dutch like to dress nicely as an expression of their personality.

Addressing People
- The Dutch don't insist on their titles, but they do take pride in them.
- First-name basis is very common in business environments.

Business Cards
- Bring enough cards. The Dutch like them.
- Make sure your card is in English and provides your title(s) and position, for the Dutch have a deep respect for academic degrees.
- Pay special attention to the cards they give you, so you know who is who, and also you might want to compliment them on theirs.

Incentives
- In the Netherlands gifts are very much appreciated. The Dutch are known for loving everything that they get for free, no matter how small.

Doing Business
- For the first meeting, you need a well-prepared agenda, and a very clear, well-structured presentation. The Dutch like to be to-the-point; even though they might take some time for small talk, the meetings will be "strictly business."
- They are very straightforward and direct, and not only in the business environment.
- They like to state the opposite of what they mean, using negative ways of talking, e.g. "nice weather again" ... while it is storming and raining.
- The Dutch do keep their promises and expect the same from you.
- When you make statements, make sure you can prove them to be true.
- The Dutch respect qualities such as honesty and being straightforward. Bluntness is preferred to deceptiveness. Constructive criticism is more useful than phony compliments

Business Meals

- Lunch and dinner are excellent opportunities for business discussions.
- Lunches will often be used for brief discussions and the food will consist of mere sandwiches, soup, or salads.
- Cocktail hour is often a must before going to dinner. Dutch will invite you to a nice pub close-by the place where you will have your dinner, or at the bar of the restaurant to socialize.
- The person who invites you for a meal is not automatically offering to pay for you. "Going Dutch" was in fact a Dutch invention.
- The Dutch are very fond of etiquette rules and disapprove of bad manners.
- Upscale restaurants expect men and women to dress very well.

Table Manners and Etiquette
- All the previous written guidelines are followed and conducted by the Dutch.

Social Events
- When walking on the street, informal dress is okay.
- Try to be punctual at all times, to both business and social events.
- For a social gathering, informal means nice casual clothes.
- Keep conversation interesting; Dutch like to talk about "hot-topics." Don't ask them their political interest; that is considered to be a private issue.
- Gifts are very welcome for social events. Flowers, plants, booze, things from your country; they like it all.
- More-precious gifts are appreciated when staying at a family's house.
- Arriving a little late at social events, is accepted but still not very nice.

First Business Encounters
- Never be late, not even one minute. If you have to be, make sure you call to tell.
- Do not look away.
- Do not give a weak handshake.
- Do not forget to compliment them on their offices, cards, etc.

Dress Code
- Do not wear casual clothes for business appointments.
- Do not overdress by wearing flashy designer clothes.

Addressing People
- Do not treat any person differently from another.
- Do not forget to shake hands with everyone; coming and going.

Business Cards
- Do not forget to have your card in English.

Incentives
- Do not forget to bring enough for everyone.

Doing Business
- Do not abruptly change the time and place for appointments.
- Do not show emotions during negotiations.
- Avoid boasting about your company, products, or yourself.
- Do not exaggerate; do not lie; do not forget to keep your promises.

Business Meals
- Do not take your aperitif to the table. Finish it before dinner is served.
- Do not start drinking until the host or hostess has proposed a toast to the entire company. A common toast is, "*proost*!"
- Do not break eye contact during the toast.
- Do not forget to inform your host upfront about special diets. The Dutch are aware of health issues and won't be offended.
- Do not presume to seat yourself.

Table Manners and Etiquette
• All the previously written guidelines still count.

Social Events
• Do not talk about private topics in public.
• Do not ask personal questions.
• Do not speak rude language in public.
• Do not come late for social appointments.
• Do not leave big amounts of food on your plate; you will offend the host.
• Do not leave the table before your host does.
• Do not leave right away after dinner.
• Do not be surprised if you see women sunbathing topless.

Belgium - BELGIË/BELGIQUE

In General
The quaint kingdom of Belgium, is divided into two parts: **Flanders and Wallonia**. Its capital is Brussels. It is bordered by the following countries: the Netherlands, Germany, Luxembourg and France. On the west side Belgium hugs a small part of the North Sea. It has a temperate maritime climate.

Due to the division of the country, it is split linguistically as well. The majority of the nation (60 percent) are Flemish (read Dutch) speakers; the Walloons are the French speakers. For a small country, though, it has produced some big names: the great painters who are still admired worldwide, Breughel, Van Dijck, and Rubens made sure that every art lover knows where Belgium is situated. Belgians are also renowned for their enjoyment of the good things in life; their chocolate has made many hearts melt worldwide. And in fact, "French fries" should be called "Belgian fries."

A Little History
The kingdom was established in 1830 after a small fight with the Netherlands, who previously owned Belgium. It is for that reason, that people in Flanders still speak Dutch. Belgium had prosperity under the French duke of Burgundy during

the 14th century. The golden age began to wear down half-way through the 15th century, when Belgium, the Netherlands, and Luxembourg were inherited by Spain. The same fate that was cast upon the Netherlands, landed upon Belgium which was a part of the Lowlands in those days: an 80-year war hurt a lot of people, but in the end Holland and its allied provinces booted out the Spaniards.

Belgium and Luxembourg stayed under Spanish rule. Napoleon's defeat at the Battle of Waterloo led to the creation of the Netherlands, connecting Belgium and Luxembourg to the Netherlands. But the Catholic Belgians revolted, winning independence in 1830. King Leopold II gained fortune by exploitation of his properties in African Congo. Germans invaded Belgium in 1914. Another German attack in 1940 saw the entire country taken over within three weeks. Postwar Belgium was characterized by an economic boom, later accentuated by Brussels's appointment as the headquarters of the European Union and the North Atlantic Treaty Organization (NATO). Belgium is now home to diplomats, and with them a highly bureaucratic form of internationalism popped up as well.

Business Profile

Belgian businesspeople are in general flexible. They show great respect for compromise and European-orientation. However, while they tend to be a bit conservative and skeptical, but their love of "the good life" drips through all their deals. Differences between the Flemish and Walloons:

The Flemish are less formal, practical, have more flat organizational structures, and are very consensus-oriented. They like delegation of authority, approachable superiors, and short lines of communication. In a non-assertive way they seek compromise.

The Walloons are more authoritarian, autocratic, hierarchical, status-conscious and decisive. They like hierarchical and formal ways, with a vertical structure and little delegation of authority. They are pretty conservative, and follow the lead of the delegation head. Personal relationships precede business relationships. Initial encounters are generally for getting acquainted and developing trust.

Agendas

Coming from **Indonesia**, where the culture prescribes modesty, the Surabayan business delegation was sitting quietly around the negotiation table in **Belgium**, waiting for the meeting to start.

Not used to all the small talk that went on, they waited patiently for the meeting to start or maybe even to continue. Their Spanish business counterparts were talking and talking and gestured a lot while they were talking all at the same time.

It was hard for the Indonesian guests to comprehend what was going on. They could not understand why their hosts did not officially start the meeting and also why they were not following the agenda.

(More on page 70.)

First Business Encounters
- Give at least one weeks notice for an appointment made by telephone; allow at least two weeks for an appointment made by mail.
- Make sure you are on time when an appointment has been scheduled.
- All Belgians shake hands with everyone both on arrival and on departure. French-speakers may kiss or embrace their acquaintances.
- Introductions consist of exchanging cards, names, etc., and offering you something to drink. Belgians like to socialize before doing business. Be prepared for a personal approach. Coffee and tea time are also important.
- Offer a firm handshake as you make eye contact.
- Shake hands with everyone, coming and going.
- Tell people your first name and family name when being introduced.

Dress Code
- Check the weather report of the country; it can be cold and rainy.
- Bring formal outfits as well as casual ones. Men wear dark suits and ties; women wear stylish suits or dresses. Belgians pay attention to details such as polished shoes and good-quality jewelry and accessories.
- You will be judged by the way you dress, so keep it simple but elegant.

Addressing People
- Belgians like their titles, but they don't insist on them.
- First-name basis depends on the other party. You will see it more in Flanders than in Wallonia. When offered, you may call them by their first name, otherwise you will have to be very polite and call them: "*mijnheer*" [sir] or "*madam*" [madam] for the Flemish-speaking part and "*monsieur*" [sir] or "*madam*" [madam] for the French-speaking part.
- Showing too much excitement or animation is usually frowned upon.
- Try to keep English as the mutual language, even when you speak French.

Business Cards
- Bring enough cards. They like them.
- Make sure your card is in English and provides your title(s) and position, for Belgians have a deep respect for academic degrees.
- When you travel to the "French part," have your card also in French.
- Pay special attention to the cards they give you, so you know who is who; also, you might want to compliment them on theirs.

Incentives
- In Belgium gifts are very rarely exchanged. When you do bring one, make sure it is something without names or logos. Specialties from your own country are welcome.

Doing Business

- For the first meeting, you need an agenda for everyone present, and a very clear, well-structured presentation. Belgians like to be to-the-point, even though they might take some time for small talk, the meetings will be: "strictly business."
- Belgians tend to be conceptual thinkers. They are willing to compromise and are firm believers in common-sense approaches and solutions
- Avoid boasting about your company, products, or yourself.
- Any request from a Belgian office means they expect a prompt reply and it is essential to assure Belgian clients that you will meet all deadlines and will be available to offer assistance when necessary.

Business Meals

- Lunch and dinner are excellent opportunities for business discussions. Belgians like to eat and do business at the same time.
- Lunches often will be used for business discussions and it sometimes will extend into the afternoon.
- Belgians are fond of the good life and take eating and drinking extremely seriously. You can expect a culinary treat, wherever you eat.
- The person who invites you for a meal is not automatically paying.
- Belgians are very fond of etiquette rules and disapprove of bad manners.
- Upscale restaurants expect men and women to dress very well.
- Take your time when you dine; Belgians are very sociable eaters and love to linger on long after the dinner is over.

Table Manners and Etiquette

- All the previous written guidelines are followed and conducted.

Social Events

- Do praise Belgium and its many achievements and especially its cuisine.
- When walking on the street, informal dress is okay.
- Try to be punctual at all times, to both business and social events.
- For a social gathering, informal means nice casual clothes.
- Hiding your hands in your pockets is seen as very rude; try to stay at least an arm's length away from the person when talking with him or her.
- Keep conversation interesting; they like to talk about their country's goodies.
- Gifts are okay for social events: flowers, liquor, or things from your country.
- More-precious gifts are welcome when you are staying at a family's house.

First Business Encounters
• Never be late, not even one minute. If you have to be late, call to tell them.
• Do not look away.

Dress Code
• Do not wear casual clothes for business appointments.
• Do not overdress by wearing flashy jewelry.

Addressing People
• Do not treat any person differently from another.
• Do not forget to shake hands with everyone; coming and going.

Business Cards
• Do not forget to have your card in English and/or French.

Incentives
• Do not bring chocolate; they think they have the best there is.

Doing business
• Do not abruptly change the time and place for appointments.
• Do not show emotions during negotiations.
• Do not exaggerate; do not lie; do not forget to keep your promises.

Business Meals
• Do not take your aperitif to the table. Finish it before dinner is served.
• Do not start drinking until the host or hostess has proposed a toast to the entire company. A common toast is, "*proost*!" or the French "*santé*."
• Do not break eye contact during the toast.
• Do not presume to seat yourself.

Table Manners and Etiquette
• All the previously written guidelines still count.

Social events
- Do not ask them about their history.
- Do not discuss linguistic divisions with Belgians.
- Do not speak French to the Flemish.
- Do not make comparisons between the Flemish and the Dutch.
- Do not make comparisons between the Walloons and the French.
- Do not speak rude language in public.
- Do not come late for social appointments.
- Do not leave big amounts of food on your plate; you will offend the host.
- Do not use your toothpick in public.
- Do not yawn in public; it is perceived as rude.
- Do not chew gum in public; it is vulgar.
- Do not crack your knuckles; it is seen as vulgar and obscene.
- Do not blow your nose in public, ever.

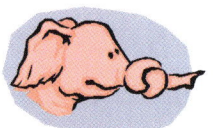

TIP
**When you come from a completely different culture it is sometimes difficult to start behaving in a different way.
However, you are always entitled to request that the participants in a meeting stick to agendas. You also have the right to ask what is going on.**

It is therefore wise to have the chairman summarize the major points discussed during the meeting. Also, you have the right to take notes, and at the end of the meeting you may verify your notes with the whole group.

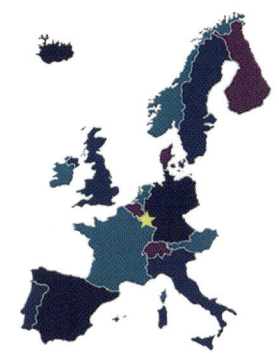

Luxembourg - LUXEMBOURGH

In General
This small landlocked country is the only grand duchy in the world. Bordered by Belgium, Germany and France; nothing is more than an hour away from its capital which has the same name as the country: Luxembourg.
The nation's motto is inscribed throughout the capital buildings:
"*Mir wëlle bleiwe wat mir sin*" which means: "We want to remain what we are".

The grand duke is the head of state and rules the constitutional monarchy. The country has a modified continental climate with mild winters and cool summers. The Moselle Valley, east of the capital, produces their famous Moselle wine.

A Little History
In 963 Count Sigefroid of Ardennes, built a castle in Luxembourg and founded a small dynasty that was fought over by many European leaders for many years. By the end of the Middle Ages, Sigefroid's city had the Burgundians, Spanish, French, Austrians and Prussians all fighting bloody battles to conquer and secure it.

Destroyed and rebuilt more than 20 times in 400 years, it grew to become the strongest fortress in Europe after Gibraltar. Listed as a French "forestry department" during Napoleon's reign, Luxembourg was included in the newly formed United Kingdom of the Netherlands (that is why they still have the same flag as the Dutch), along with Belgium, in 1814. Sixteen years later, when Belgium liberated itself from the Netherlands (confiscating a large part of Luxembourg), Luxembourg's desire for independence grew stronger, and in 1830 it became the Grand Duchy of Luxembourg which proclaimed neutrality.

Overrun by Germany in both World Wars, it ended its neutrality in 1948 when it joined the Benelux Customs Union and NATO the following year. By 1957 Luxembourg had developed into an active member of the European governing bodies and was one of the European Union's architects. The country's identity is quite similar to its neighbors.' Multilingualism is universal; both German and French are used in daily life.

Business Profile

The Luxembourg business profile is a lot like the German: very hierarchical. However, they do take some from the French as well: they can be very charming. The business persons behave very formally; they love their titles and like to show off their "good breeding." Personal matters are never discussed with colleagues, no matter how friendly they are with one another outside the office.

Decisions are made at the top of the company and in private. It may take a while until a decision has been made because Luxembourgers study both the long-term as well as the immediate effects of a decision. Things move rather slowly, so you'd better show some patience and try to avoid confrontational behavior and stay away from high-pressure tactics.

Luxembourgers treat their business opponents with the utmost respect and expect the same behavior in return. Here is what you should and shouldn't do in order to smooth the path toward doing business successfully.

Ladies First?

"My mother has taught me that ladies always come first," said the **Brazilian** businessman. "On one of my business trips to **Luxembourg**, I had to take my business counterpart, a very nice lady, out to dinner. When we arrived at the door of the restaurant, I opened the door to let her enter first. To my surprise she hesitated and didn't want to go in. I asked her if anything was wrong. She smiled, said nothing and went in. What did I do wrong?"

Yes, of course ladies go first. But there are two exceptions. Never, ever let a lady enter "first" in a restaurant or bar. The gentleman has to enter first to check out the safety of the place (there might be drunks or bad company). And you never let a lady go first on stairs; you might be able to get a glimpse of her legs when she is wearing a skirt, and that also is not done.

First Business Encounters
- It is recommended that you get a third-party introduction to a business.
- Give at least one or two weeks' notice for an appointment made by telephone; allow at least a month for an appointment made by mail.
- Business introductions consist of exchanging cards, names and titles.
- Offer a firm brief handshake as you make brief eye contact.
- Shake hands with everyone, upon coming and going.
- Tell your family name, titles and function/position upon introduction.
- Luxembourgers take pride in their country and culture, so you might want to say something nice about it.

Dress Code
- Check the weather report of the country.
- Men wear elegant suits and ties; women wear fashionable suits or skirts. Casual attire is not allowed in businesses.

Addressing People
- Luxembourgers insist on their titles; address them accordingly.
- First-name basis is not common in business environments.
- When you speak French, always use the formal way of addressing: "*vous*," and the honorific titles: "*Madame*" or "*Monsieur*."

Business Cards
- Bring enough cards.
- Have your card in English and French with your title(s) and position on it.
- Pay special attention to the cards they give you, so you know who is who, and you also might want to compliment them on theirs.

Incentives
- Gifts are appreciated as long as they show some class; e.g., a nice pen or a picture book from your country.

Doing Business
- For the first meeting, you need a well-prepared agenda, and a very clear, well-structured presentation. Luxembourgers like to be to-the-point, the meetings will be, "strictly business."
- Meetings follow a very strict timetable.
- Wait until the host (business counterpart) invites you to be seated.
- They are very direct, and not only in the business environment.
- Luxembourgers keep their promises and expect the same from you.

- When you make statements, make sure you can prove them to be true. Luxembourgers like to see facts.
- Avoid boasting about your company, products, or yourself, Luxembourgers see that as a sign of "poor breed".
- They also respect qualities such as honesty and straightforwardness. However, bluntness is absolutely unaccepted.

Business Meals
- Lunch and dinner are possible opportunities for business discussions.
- Lunches will often be used for brief discussions and the food will consist of mere sandwiches, soup or salads.
- Upscale restaurants expect men and women to dress very well.
- Wait to be seated.
- See the section on "France" for more details.

Table Manners and Etiquette
- All the previous written guidelines are strictly followed.

Social Events
- When walking on the street, informal dress is okay.
- Be punctual at all times, to both business and social events.
- For a social gathering, informal means nice casual clothes.
- Keep conversation general. Try culture, sports, art, etc., for topics.
- Gifts are acceptable for social events.
- More-precious gifts are appreciated when you are staying at a family's house.

First Business Encounters
- Never be late, not even one minute. If you have to be late, make sure you call to apologize and explain why you will be late.
- Do not forget to mention their titles.
- Do not engage in small talk.

Dress Code
- Do not wear casual clothes for business appointments.
- Do not overdress by wearing flashy designer clothes and jewelry.
- Do not take your jacket off during any business encounter.

Addressing People
- Do not forget to mention their titles.
- Do not forget to shake hands with everyone.

Business Cards
- Do not forget to have your card in English and French.

Incentives
- Do not bring a gift for the first encounter.

Doing Business
- Do not abruptly change the time, and place for appointments.
- Do not be late for meetings, not even one minute.
- Do not sit down, until you are invited to do so.
- Do not show emotions during negotiations.
- Do not take your jacket off during meetings.
- Do not interrupt a meeting, for what ever reason.
- Do not try to force a decision.
- Do not be impatient or confrontational.

Business Meals
- Do not take your aperitif to the table. Finish it before dinner is served.
- Do not start drinking until the host or hostess has proposed a toast to the entire company.
- Do not break eye contact during the toast.
- Do not forget to inform your host upfront about special diets.
- Do not presume to seat yourself.

Table Manners and Etiquette
- All the previously written guidelines still count.

Social Events

- Do not forget to show good manners at all times.
- Do not talk about private topics in public.
- Do not backslap, hug or kiss, or touch Luxembourgers in public.
- Do not ask personal questions.
- Do not speak rude language in public.
- Do not come late for social appointments.
- Do not forget to bring flowers (odd numbers and no chrysanthemums) or chocolates for the hostess.
- Do not sit down before your host does.
- Do not forget to return a toast to your host.
- Do not forget to show your table manners.
- Do not leave big amounts of food on your plate; you will offend the host.
- Do not leave the table before your host does.
- Do not leave right away after dinner.

Germany - DEUTSCHLAND

In General
Germany (its capital is Berlin) bridges maritime western and continental eastern Europe, and warm southern and cool northern Europe. It is bordered by the North Sea and Baltic Sea coasts in the north. Bordering countries are (clockwise): Denmark, Poland, the Czech Republic, Austria, Switzerland, France, Luxembourg, Belgium, and the Netherlands. The Federal Republic of Germany is a democracy with a liberal free-market economy, freedom of religion and freedom of the press. Germany is a member of the European Union (EU). Check the weather report of the region before you visit, so you know what to expect.

A Little History
Germany's history is one of ups and downs. All of Europe's great empires have tried to conquer Germany, with little success. By the time the house of Habsburg took control in the 13th century, it was little more than a conglomerate of German-speaking states run by parochial princes. In 1866 Otto von Bismarck, chancellor of Prussia, annexed most of Germany. The Prussian king Wilhelm I was installed as emperor, "*Kaiser*", and a united Germany was born for the first time. Wilhelm II ruled long enough to lead Germany into WWI, and then came Adolf Hitler and WWII which ended in 1945 and divided Germany into East and West. During the following 25 years West Germany became prosperous while East Germany suffered. The destruction of the Berlin Wall in 1989 reunified Germany to the country it is today. Germany is known for its beer and some real nice cars.
Isn't it every boy's (and man's) dream to own a Porsche, a BMW, or a Mercedes, once they have grown up?

Business Profile
Germans businesspeople are "*gründlich und pünktlich*," meaning that they rely on their punctuality, desire for perfection, and love of law and order. They are also known for their criticism and lack of diplomacy. But they honor their traditions and privacy. Being funny is not really appreciated in a business setting. It is true that Germans can be rigid, fixed, and outdated. Hierarchy is a necessity in German businesses, which results in excessive respect shown to one's superiors.

The German manager concentrates intensely on two objectives: product quality and product service. He wants his company to be the best, and he wants it to have the best products.

Their organizations follow structured and vertical lines. Germans are very formal, and appear well-dressed, disciplined, and serious in their business surroundings. They prefer to use their own language for negotiations, and will often reveal their emotions in body language or with facial expressions.

Germans treat their business opponents with respect and expect the same behavior from them. In comparison with other Europeans, Germans are very conscientious of hierarchy and always show deep respect for their superiors.

Professional rank and status are determined by the personal achievements. Therefore, if you come from a highly hierarchical culture (Africa, the Far East, South America, or the Middle East), be prepared to meet a woman or younger person who has the highest rank. Always show respect, even if it is not in your culture to treat women with respect.

Bridging Communications

Determined to do business successfully, an **Argentinean** CEO and his staff went to a **German** company to try to get the exclusive rights to one of their products. They were well prepared and did a lot of "homework," so they knew what to expect. But somewhere during the second round of negotiations, communication between the two parties did not seem to click anymore.

No matter what the Argentineans tried, the Germans kept changing the subject, which resulted in a huge misunderstanding. At the end of that meeting the puzzled Argentineans went home "empty handed". They later found out that the company, they were dealing with, had gone bankrupt.

(More on page 82.)

First Business Encounters
- Give at least one or two weeks' notice for an appointment made by telephone; allow at least a month for an appointment made by mail.
- Be prepared to make an appointment for most things. Making appointments for a more-detailed telephone conversation is also not unusual.
- Never underestimate the importance of punctuality in German business culture. Arriving even 5 or 10 minutes late is perceived as too late.
- German business introductions consist of a very formal exchange of cards, names, etc. If you are sitting and being introduced to a new contact or associate, be sure to stand up before extending your hand.
- Offer a firm handshake, and make brief eye contac, coming and going.
- In very formal business environments, the highest-ranking person enters the room first, regardless of gender or age.
- Tell people your title, first name and family name when being introduced.
- Any effort to use some basic German words will be appreciated. Such as, *Vielen Dank*: [Thank you very much]; *Guten Tag/Abend*: [Good morning/evening]; *Auf Wiedersehen*: [Till we meet again].

Dress Code
- Check the weather report of the region before you visit Germany.
- Bring formal outfits as well as casual ones. Men wear dark suits and white shirts and simple ties. Women wear conservative suits or skirts. Casual attire is only allowed for the lower-ranked personnel.

Addressing People
- Germans insist on their titles, especially the older generation. When you meet a person with a title, you will have to address him or her accordingly, e.g., *Mr. Dieter von Amsberg* who is also a doctor, will have to be called, *Herr Doktor Von Amsberg*. If the person is a woman, you will have to say, *Frau Doktor Von Amsberg*.
- First name basis is very uncommon. Even colleagues address each other with "*Herr*" and "*Frau*."
- When you speak German, always address people the formal way. Use the formal "*Sie*" (you). The informal "*Du*" (you) is for younger people.

Business Cards
- Bring enough cards. Germans like them.
- Make sure your card is in English and provides all academic information you have, including your title(s) and position.
- Pay special attention to the cards they give you, so you know how to address them. Make sure you use the proper titles before saying their names.

Incentives
- In Germany a small gift is polite, especially when contacts are made for the first time. Tasteful office items with your company logo are okay.
- Avoid bringing expensive gifts, especially in the eastern part of Germany.

Doing Business
- For the first meeting you need a well-prepared agenda. Germans are schedule-oriented; no small talk before meetings. Expect their business communication to be very agenda-based. Germans are analytical thinkers, requiring lots of facts and examples from you.
- Germans are very straightforward and direct, especially in the business environment.
- Germans might appear distant and unfriendly, but in fact that is their business attitude. They separate personal and business relations very strictly.

Business Meals
- Lunch is the primary meal for business discussions.
- Germans do not often make business decisions during dinner. Wait for your German dining companions to initiate any discussions about business.
- The person who invites you for a meal is not automatically paying.
- Upscale restaurants expect men and women to dress very well.
- Have some food in your stomach before you go drinking with Germans for you can expect some very strong liquor to be offered to you when you're having cocktails. Germans are proud of their "*Schnapps*", little shots of potent alcoholic beverages.
- After the toast: "*Prosit,*" they wish you good appetite: "*Guten Appetit.*"

Table Manners and Etiquette
- All the previous written guidelines are acknowledged in Germany.

Social Events
- When walking on the street, informal dress is okay.
- Be punctual at all times, to both business and social events.
- For a social gathering, informal means nice casual clothes.
- Keep conversation general. Try culture, sports, art, etc., for topics.
- Gifts are acceptable for social events. If you bring flowers, don't bring roses.
- More-precious gifts are appreciated when you are staying at a family's house.

First Business Encounters
- Never be late, not even one minute. If you are late, make sure you call tell them.
- Do not forget to mention their titles.
- Do not engage in small talk.

Dress Code
- Do not wear casual clothes for business appointments.
- Do not overdress by wearing flashy designer clothes and jewelry.

Addressing People
- Do not treat any person differently from another.
- Do not forget to shake hands with everyone.

Business Cards
- Do not forget to have your card in English.

Incentives
- Do not bring a gift for the first encounter.

Doing Business
- Do not abruptly change the time and place for appointments.
- Do not show emotions during negotiations.
- Do not feel intimidated by all their titles; it is part of their show.
- Do not use your cell phone during meetings.

Business Meals
- Do not take your aperitif to the table. Finish it before dinner is served.
- Do not start drinking until the host or hostess has proposed a toast to the entire company.
- Do not break eye contact during the toast.
- Do not wish them, "*Mahlzeit,*" it is rude; use the polite way: "*Guten Appetit.*"
- Do not forget to inform your host upfront about special diets. German food is rather heavy on the stomach.
- Do not presume to seat yourself.

Table Manners and Etiquette
- All the previously written guidelines still count.

Social Events
- Do not talk about private topics in public.
- Do not talk about the World Wars.
- Do not backslap, hug or kiss, or touch a German in public.
- Do not ask personal questions.
- Do not speak rude language in public.
- Do not come late for social appointments.
- Do not leave big amounts of food on your plate; you will offend the host.
- Do not leave the table before your host does.
- Do not leave right away after dinner.

TIP

Germans are very proud people. They don't like to lose face and they do know how to "bridge" topics.

 This tactic is often used, when people want to steer communications into a different direction.
It is a simple tactic and consists merely of a couple of phrases:

"That is a very interesting proposal, which reminds me of this other subject that needs to be discussed first!"

"We had the same suggestion a week ago from company X, and had to reject it because this company ...."
(and the rest of the discussion is about the other company).

What you should do when you notice that people are trying to **"bridge"** you away from your mission is to tell them, that you are really interested in that particular topic, but that you prefer to finish the discussion as it was started. In other words, stick to the agenda.

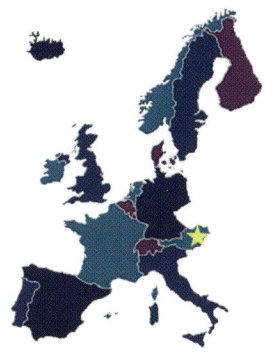

Austria - ÖSTERREICH

In General
This landlocked country in the heart of Europe is bordered in the north by Germany and (clockwise) further on by the Czech Republic, Hungary, Slovenia, Italy, and Switzerland. Due to its mountainous parts and large forests, it has various types of weather; year round. Austria (its capital is Vienna or "*Wien*") has a gorgeous musical tradition. Didn't we all waltz once on Johann Strauss's music (The Blue Danube) and don't we all enjoy the great compositions of Mozart?

In this fairy-tale country, many people still wear their traditional costumes, which truly make them look like fairy-tale figurines. The men in their *Lederhosen* (short leather pants) and the women in the cutest *Dirndl Kleider* (doll dresses) seem to have let the time go past them as they stroll around in their quaint little mountain villages, or pick Edelweiss and herd their cattle on the snow-peaked mountain slopes in the summer.

A Little History

Austria has seen many different tribes occupy its territories: Celts, Romans, Huns, and Slavs, they all came and went. Charlemagne established a territory in the Danube Valley, known as the Ostmark in 803. The area became predominantly Germanic in 955, when it was conquered by the Germans.

By 1278 the Habsburgs had gained control and this mighty dynasty managed to rule Austria right up until World War I. The Habsburgians became emperors of Germany in 1438. They acquired in 1526 the kingdoms of Hungary and Bohemia.

As a result of the Napoleonic Wars, the Habsburgian possessions became independent in 1804, as the Empire of Austria. Rivalry between Prussia and Austria inside Germany, resulted in 1866 in the defeat of Austria: it was forced to leave the German confederation. Austria was restyled in 1867 into Austria-Hungary.

After World War I Austria-Hungary was dissolved and the Republics of Hungary, German-Austria, and Czech(o)Slovakia became separate states. The post-war settlement defined the nation's borders and created a republic, but the history of modern Austria begins in 1955, when Austria became an independent, sovereign republic and joined the United Nations. Austria has been a member of the European Union since 1995 and is one of the member states, that hold the euro as its currency.

Famous for its Swarovski crystal and *Sachertorte* (delicious chocolate cake), Austria also had one of its poets and writers, Elfriede Jelinek, awarded a Nobel Prize in literature in 2004.

Business Profile
Relatively few Austrians speak much English, outside the senior management of multinational companies and/or in the larger cities. Even competent English-speakers prefer to communicate in German whenever possible. Meetings are not brainstorming sessions and it is not considered important to reach a consensus. Austrians hate wasting time; the senior person takes the chair and controls the agenda.

Meetings end abruptly, when the chairman reaches the end of the agenda. It is still rare to find women in senior management positions in Austria, though they are better represented in professions such as law. Also, in Austria it is a lot about who you know, to get to the right person or place.

First Business Encounters
- Give at least three to four weeks' notice for an appointment.
- Austrians are very punctual and expect the same from their visitors.
- Offer a firm handshake as you make brief eye contact.
- Shake hands with everyone, coming and going.
- Tell people your first name and family name.
- Austrians like to hear about your trip upon arrival; they welcome anyone who shows some knowledge of their country. They take pride in their country, so you might want to say something nice about it.

Dress Code
- Check the weather report of the country; it can be cold and rainy.
- Bring formal outfits as well as casual ones. Men wear suits and ties; women wear nice outfits.
- Dress simply but elegantly. In order to make that crucial first impression, you should wear only high-quality clothing and polished leather shoes.

Addressing People
- Use the courtesy titles, "*Herr*" [sir, or mister], or "*Frau*" [madam] followed by the family name, until invited to do otherwise.
- First-name basis is not very common in business environments.
- Austrians insist on their titles; be sure always to use them.
- They tend to follow the same etiquette rules regarding this topic as the Germans. But don't ever tell them that; they feel that is an insult.

Business Cards
- Bring enough cards. Austrians expect you to give them to everybody.
- Have your cards translated into German on one side.
- Status is important in Austria; therefore, your company position should appear clearly beneath your title, name, and academic/professional qualifications, for Austrians have a deep respect for academic degrees.
- Pay special attention to the cards they give you, so you know who is who, and you also might want to compliment them on theirs.

Incentives
- Only give a present, if you have received one first.
- Bring something tasteful from your own country.
- Presents have to be opened right away, so you can show appreciation.

Doing Business
- For the first meeting you need a well-prepared agenda, and a very clear, well-structured presentation, preferably in German.

- If you don't speak German, it is advisable to have an interpreter on hand.
- They take time for small talk, but meetings will be "strictly business."
- Have your facts and figures available in the form of a point-by-point printed handout to reinforce your presentation.
- Austrians are very straightforward and direct, and not only in the business.
- Austrians do keep their promises and expect the same from you.
- When you make statements, make sure you can prove them to be true.
- Decision-making can be slow because Austrians tend to be risk averse, and make decisions methodically with tremendous precision. Be patient.
- The Austrians respect qualities such as honesty and straightforwardness.
- Respect, conservatism, and a respect for conservatism are the keys to business success in Austria.

Business Meals
- Lunch and dinner are opportunities for business discussions.
- Business lunches will be the largest meal of the day.
- Wait for your host to bring up the topic of business, but be prepared to have some pleasant "small talk" first that has nothing to do with business.
- Business dinners will be preceded by drinks and appetizers.
- After dinner, continue the conversation over coffee and brandy or liqueurs.
- Try to leave within an hour of the end of the meal.
- The person who invites you for a meal, is not automatically paying.
- Upscale restaurants expect men and women to dress very well.

Table Manners and Etiquette
- All the previous written guidelines are acknowledged, with one extension: you should acknowledge everyone you meet with a formal greeting, before engaging in conversation. The most common salutation is: "*Grüß Gott*" [literally, "greet God," but it is used as "good day"].

Social Events
- When walking on the street, informal dress is okay.
- Be punctual at all times, to both business and social events.
- For a social gathering, informal means nice casual clothes.
- Keep conversation general. Try culture, sports, art, etc., for topics.
- Courtesy and an almost exaggerated politeness have to become part of your business attitude.
- Gifts are acceptable for social events.
- More-precious gifts are appreciated, when you are staying at a family's house.

First Business Encounters
- Never be late, not even one minute. If you have to be late, call to tell them.
- Do not forget to mention their titles.

Dress Code
- Do not wear casual clothes for business appointments.
- Do not overdress by wearing flashy designer clothes and jewelry.

Addressing People
- Do not treat any person differently from another.
- Do not forget to shake hands with everyone.

Business Cards
- Do not forget to have your card in German as well.

Incentives
- Do not be the first one to give a gift

Doing Business
- Do not abruptly change the time and place for appointments.
- Do not show emotions during negotiations.

Business Meals
- Do not start drinking until the host or hostess has proposed a toast to the entire company. A common toast is, "*Prost!*"
- Do not break eye contact during the toast.
- Do not begin eating until the signal has been given; this is usually an exchange of "*Guten Appetit!*" [Enjoy your meal], initiated by the host or hostess.
- Do not forget to inform your host upfront about special diets. Austrian food is rather heavy on the stomach.
- Do not take large portions of food if you are not certain you can eat it all, as you will be perceived as wasteful.
- Do not presume to seat yourself.

Table Manners and Etiquette
- All the previously written guidelines still count, with one extension, do NOT use a knife to cut your food; you should cut your food with the side of your fork. Using a knife implies that you think that the food is not tender enough, and this is considered "poor manners."

Social Events

- Do not talk about private topics in public.
- Do not backslap, hug or kiss, or touch an Austrian in public.
- Do not ask personal questions.
- Do not speak rude language in public.
- Do not come late for social appointments.
- Do not exaggerate and give extravagant compliments.
- Do not bring roses if you want to bring flowers. Roses are considered to be for lovers only.

Switzerland -
CONFÖDERATIO HELVETICA
Suisse/Schweiz/Svizzera
(French)   (German)   (Italian)

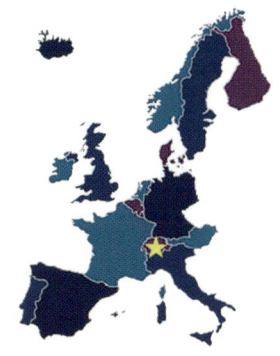

In General
This interesting, relatively small landlocked country has four different names, as you can see, due to its neighboring countries. Its capital is Bern. It is bordered by Germany, Liechtenstein, Austria, Italy, and France. Its climate is temperate, but due to the many beautiful mountains it varies with altitude, cold, cloudy, rainy/snowy winters; cool to warm, cloudy, humid summers with occasional showers. The country has also four languages: German, French, Italian, and Romansch. It will not surprise you to see street or city names posted in all four languages.

The unity of the Swiss Confederation is portrayed in the legend of the famous William Tell. But that story is not the only thing that became wellknown. How about the famous Swiss chocolates, cheese fondue, or their special way of singing, called "yodeling?" And of course their famous "bank secrecy."

A Little History
The first inhabitants of the region were a Celtic tribe, the Helvetia. The Romans appeared on the scene in 107 B.C. Then the Swiss tried territorial expansion and gained independence from the Holy Roman emperor Maximilian I in 1499. While the rest of Europe was fighting in the Thirty Years War, the Swiss closed ranks and stayed neutral. At the end of the war in 1648 they were recognized in the Treaty of Westphalia as a neutral state. Nevertheless, the French Republic invaded Switzerland in 1798 and created the Helvetica Republic.

However, the Congress of Vienna guaranteed Switzerland's independence and permanent neutrality in 1815. In 1848 a new federal constitution was agreed on and it is still in place today.

Switzerland's independence and neutrality have long been honored by the major European powers and Switzerland was not involved in either of the two World Wars. The country became a UN member in 2002.

Business Profile

Generally speaking, the German and French Swiss are conceptual, analytical thinkers; the Italian Swiss think more associatively. The German and French Swiss often have a tendency to use universal rules to solve problems, while the Italian Swiss usually prefer to become personally involved in each situation. For more-detailed information, you will have to read all about them on their own "home" country pages.

In all cases, nationalism and utopian ideals influence their ways. In Swiss business culture, there is a reluctance to take risks. Also, few women hold high-level positions; they must work much harder than their male colleagues to achieve a comparable level of success.

The Swiss treat their business opponents with respect and a bit of arrogance, but they only want respect in return. You might want to read the French, Italian or German business profiles, when you know in what region you will be. It is more than likely that you will encounter much of what is written there when visiting a specific region. Here is, in general, what you should and shouldn't do in order to smooth the path toward doing business successfully.

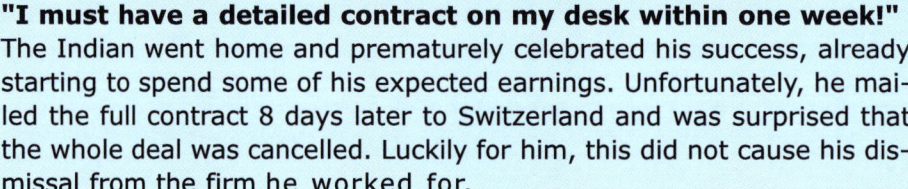

Listening and Verifying

During the final negotiations on a million-dollar order in a **Swiss** engine factory, the visiting **Indian** sales man from Calcutta was already showing happiness because of the successful transaction. The Swiss CEO gave him specific instructions and terms on which his Indian counterpart had to act; otherwise, NO DEAL. One of the terms said,
"I must have a detailed contract on my desk within one week!"
The Indian went home and prematurely celebrated his success, already starting to spend some of his expected earnings. Unfortunately, he mailed the full contract 8 days later to Switzerland and was surprised that the whole deal was cancelled. Luckily for him, this did not cause his dismissal from the firm he worked for.

Interesting detail: Following this, all of the personnel of the Indian and Swiss companies were trained in listening skills, because both CEOs acknowledged the importance of truly listening and understanding the conversation. (More on page 94.)

First Business Encounters
- Give at least one month's notice for an appointment.
- You should arrive at least 15 minutes earlier than the agreed-upon time.
- Punctuality is necessary on all occasions, whether business or social, especially in the German speaking part of Switzerland.
- Swiss business introductions consist of exchanging cards, names, etc.
- Offer a firm handshake as you make brief eye contact.
- Shake hands with everyone, coming and going.
- Tell people your first name and family name, when being introduced.
- Be formal and polite at all times.
- Praise the country and its achievements.

Dress Code
- Check the weather report of the region you are about to visit.
- Bring formal outfits as well as casual ones.
- Men wear suits and silk ties; women wear elegant suits or skirts.
- All clothes for both men and women should be subdued in appearance, and more subdued in the German than in the French and Italian regions.
- Dress modestly; any jewelry should be elegant but understated.

Addressing People
- Address the Swiss by their professional or courtesy title, followed by their surname.
- First-name basis is not very common in business environments.
- Check the German, French and Italian chapters on these topics.

Business Cards
- Bring enough cards; the Swiss like them.
- Make sure your card is in English and provides your title(s) and position, for the Swiss have a deep respect for your rank within the corporate hierarchy.
- Also include the founding date of your company; the Swiss like stability and have respect for a well-established company.
- When arriving, give your card to the receptionist and/or secretary to keep on file, and then to everyone else you meet in the company!

Incentives
- Wait until the end of negotiations before presenting a gift.
- Allow your contact to give the first gift, so that you can return the gesture.
- Appropriate gifts are: books of your home country, fine wine, or whiskey.

Doing Business

- For the first meeting you need a well-prepared agenda, and a very clear, well-structured presentation. The Swiss like to be to-the-point; the meetings will be, "strictly business." German Swiss will usually get right down to business.
- They do keep their promises and expect the same from you.
- Make sure you can prove your statements to be true. They want to see facts.
- Business is considered to be very serious and humor has no place in negotiations.
- Avoid boasting about your company, products, or yourself; the Swiss real don't like that; they are not impressed by superlatives.

Business Meals
- Lunch and dinner are excellent opportunities for business discussions.
- Lunch is the main meal of the day, and business lunches are often informal.
- Lunches will often be used for brief discussions, and the food will consist of a three-course meal including dessert and fruit.
- Business dinners are occasions for formality and fine dining.
- Upscale restaurants expect men and women to dress very well.
- You have to seat yourself, after your host has taken his place.

Table Manners and Etiquette
- All the previous written guidelines are acknowledged in Switzerland.

Social Events
- When walking on the street, informal dress is okay.
- Be punctual at all times, to both business and social events.
- For a social gathering, informal means nice casual clothes.
- Keep conversation general. Try culture, history, nature, art, etc. for topics.
- Gifts are acceptable for social events.
- More-precious gifts are appreciated, when you're staying at a family's house.

First Business Encounters
- Never be late, not even one minute. If you have to be late, call to tell them.
- Do not forget to mention their titles.

Dress Code
- Do not wear casual clothes for business appointments.
- Do not overdress by wearing flashy designer clothes and jewelry.

Addressing People
- Do not treat any person differently from another.
- Do not forget to shake hands with everyone.
- Do not talk about personal issues.
- Do not make jokes; they might interpret it as mockery.
- Don't talk about military topics.

Business Cards
- Do not forget to have your card in English.

Incentives
- Do not bring a gift for the first meeting.
- Do not give knives, scissors, or any other sharp object; they imply the end of a relation and of a friendship.
- Do not give chocolates; the Swiss think their chocolate is the best in the world.

Doing Business
- Do not abruptly change the time and place for appointments.
- Do not show emotions during negotiations.

Business Meals
- Do not take your aperitif to the table. Finish it before dinner is served.
- Do not start drinking until the host or hostess has proposed a toast to the entire company.
- Clink glasses with everyone at the table, or at least those within your reach. Only then may you take your first sip.
- Do not break eye contact during the toast.
- Do not talk about business until your host starts.

Table Manners and Etiquette
• All the previously written guidelines still count.

Social Events

• Do not talk about private topics in public.
• Do not backslap, hug or kiss, or touch a Swiss in public.
• Do not ask personal questions.
• Do not speak rude language in public.
• Do not come late for social appointments.
• Do not bring chrysanthemums, lilies, or red roses.
• Do not leave large amounts of food on your plate; you will offend the host.
• Do not leave the table before your host does.
• Do not leave right away after dinner.

TIP
It is so important to listen well and to verify everything you are talking about and that you agree on. It is okay to ask permission to record conclusions so you can listen to them again. Most important, however, is to VERIFY.

One week, is 7 days, and not 8 days.

Don't think of the weekend as "non-business" days.
Try to specify "vague" terms such as: shortly, soon, etc., and use concrete dates and times. That narrows the possibilities of failure drastically.

"Shortly?
Do you mean within the next half hour?"
"Soon?
Do you mean this coming Friday or Monday next week, and at what time?"

France - FRANCE

In General
The republic of "La douce France" (its capital is Paris) borders Belgium, Luxembourg, Germany, Swiss, and Italy, in the south the Mediterranean Sea, Spain, and the Bay of Biscay, and more to the north the English Channel southeast of the UK.

France is the biggest country of western Europe and has a mixed climate: generally cool winters and mild summers overall, but mild winters and hot summers along the Mediterranean Sea. It is said, that you can live, "like a god in France". The country has a lot that you can enjoy, and it is very famous for its fine wines, great cognac, delicious champagne, but most of all for its refined cuisine. Apart from that, France is known for creating exquisite perfumes and famous fashion. Worldwide many women love to dress in Dior or Chanel creations. As stated previously, etiquette originates in France; therefore, it is advisable that you should follow the French example, without asking questions. It makes you wonder about the old saying, "When in Rome, do as the Romans do".

A Little History
France was one of the first countries to grow from feudalism to the nation-state. During the reign of Louis XIV, at the end of the 17th century, France was the dominant power in Europe. But the military campaigns of Louis and his successors led to big financial problems in the 18th century. Deteriorating economic conditions and resentment against the wealthy nobility and clerics were the principal causes of the French Revolution at the end of the 18th century.

Although the revolutionaries advocated "*liberté, égalité et fraternité*" [freedom, equality and brotherhood], France reverted to constitutional monarchy four times during the empire of the infamous Napoleon, Louis XVIII, Louis-Philippe, and the second empire of Napoleon III.

Many wars followed, but in the meantime the French also participated in colonizing countries in Africa and Indochina. It was during the days of the 4th Republic, that France had to cope with big-time trouble in Indochina and Algeria. In 1958, the government structure collapsed and General Charles de Gaulle prevented civil war. He became prime minister in June 1958 (at the beginning of the Fifth Republic) and was elected president in December of that year.

From then on, France continued to revere its rich history and independence. French leaders are increasingly tying the future of France to the continued development of the European Union. The one blemish on their "good name," remains the fact that they are conducting experiments with atomic bombs in the South Pacific.

Business Profile

French businesspeople are very fond of their culture, good manners, fashion and style. They have a reputation for being somewhat formal and rather chauvinistic. But they do have that special feeling for, "*savoir vivre,*" [know how to live] which shows in their business ethics. French managers are cautious and precise, but you may expect personal views to influence negotiations and business dealings. Decisions will not be made during meetings. Hierarchy is formal, steep, and rigid.

Surnames and formal introductions are used, politeness is essential, and respect for authority must be immediate and complete. Decision making is usually done by one person in the organization. The French workplace is highly organized and structured. Bureaucracy and administrative procedures are considered far more important than efficiency or flexibility. They like to negotiate in French, and love to get compliments about their country.

First Business Encounters
- Ensure that you make appointments for both business and social occasions.
- You will not be considered late, if you arrive ten minutes after the scheduled time. There is an increased tolerance for arriving late as you go further south.
- Give at least one or two weeks' notice for an appointment made by telephone; allow at least a month for an appointment made by regular mail.
- French business introductions consist of exchanging cards, formal introductions, names, etc.
- Offer a firm handshake as you make brief eye contact.
- Shake hands with everyone, coming and going.
- Tell people your first name and family name.
- Avoid making personal inquiries in the course of a conversation during first introductions.

Dress Code
- Check the weather report of the region you will be visiting.
- The French will perceive the way you dress as a reflection of your social status and success.
- The French love to dress formally; both men and women, whether in business or social situations.
- Wear only conservative clothing of the highest quality.
- Men should wear dark suits, particularly during the winter and when visiting the north.
- Women are advised to dress simply and with elegance. Accessorizing, which adds flair to even very simple outfits, is also widely practiced here.
- Bring formal outfits as well as casual ones.

Addressing People
- Men should be addressed as "*Monsieur*" [mister, sir] and women as "*Madame*."
- When you speak French, use "*vous*" [formal "you"], until you are asked to use the informal "you" = "*tu.*"
- The French sometimes introduce themselves by first saying their surname, followed by their first name. You may want to verify which name to use.
- They like you to try to speak a bit of French; entering an office or restaurant, you can say "*bonjour*" [good morning], or "*bonsoir*" [good evening], and "*au revoir*" [till I see you again] upon leaving. A very polite thing to do is to express gratitude for practically every thing, by using the French words: "*merci bien*" [thank you very much].
- First name basis is not very common in business environments.

Business Cards

- Bring enough cards.
- Make sure your card is also in French and provides your title(s).
- Your card should also indicate your position in French and your university degree, when it is at the Ph.D. level.
- Pay special attention to the cards they give you, so you know who is who, and you also might want to compliment them on theirs.

Incentives
- In France, giving gifts is acceptable, but exercise discretion and never add your business card.
- Gifts are expected for social events, especially as a "thank-you" after a dinner party.

Doing Business

- For the first meeting you need a well-prepared agenda, and a very clear, well-structured presentation.
- Address your message to the appropriate person in the organization.
- In the middle of an argument, they may change the subject; these digressions are characteristic and sometimes influence the final decision.
- Despite the passionate tone of business discussions, don't make the mistake of insisting that everyone agrees with your opinion, or attempt the "hard sell."
- French business protocol requires constant formality and reserve in negotiations. Trying to convince your French counterparts to "lighten up" is inappropriate.
- Refrain from discussing personal matters during negotiations.
- The French tend to be preoccupied with examining every detail before making a decision. Be prepared for a long wait before you receive an answer.
- When you make statements, make sure you can prove them to be true.
- Avoid boasting about your company, products, or yourself.
- The French respect qualities like honesty and being straightforward.

Business Meals
- Lunches are excellent opportunities for business discussions.
- Actual business, however, is not supposed to be conducted during lunch or dinner. If business has to be discussed, wait until dessert is served.
- A business lunch is a formal event starting with an appetizer, followed by a main course, cheese, dessert, and coffee.

- Dinner starts usually at 8:30 p.m., and you are expected to stay at least until 11:00 p.m.
- The person that invites you for the meal or drink, is expected to pay.
- Upscale restaurants expect men and women to dress very well.

Table Manners and Etiquette
- All the previous written guidelines are strictly followed by their French inventors.

Social Events
- When walking on the street, informal dress is okay.
- Try to be punctual at all times, to both business and social events.
- For a social gathering, informal means nice casual clothes.
- Keep conversation general. Try culture, sports, art, etc., for topics.
- Do compare France favorably to its neighbors England, Germany, Spain and Italy.
- Gifts are acceptable for social events. If you bring flowers, don't bring roses.
- More-precious gifts are appreciated, when you are staying at a family's house.
- French people are pretty physical, meaning they like to touch, hug, kiss, and embrace. You don't have to copy them, but expect them to stand very close to you when talking with you.

First Business Encounters
- Never be late, not one minute. If you have to be late, call to tell them.
- Do not forget to knock on the door before entering a room.
- Do not forget to mention their titles.

Dress Code
- Do not wear casual clothes for business appointments.

Addressing People
- Do not forget to shake hands with everyone.

Business Cards
- Do not forget to have your card in French.

Incentives
- Do not bring a very precious gift for the first meeting.
- Do not include your business card with the present.

Doing Business
- Do not abruptly change the time and place for appointments.
- Do not display familiarity or be overly friendly during business.
- Do not be impatient during meetings.
- Do not feel intimidated by all their digressions; it's important to them.

Business Meals
- Do not take your aperitif to the table. Finish it before dinner is served.
- Do not start drinking until the host or hostess has proposed a toast to the entire company and do not break eye contact during the toast.
- Do not presume to seat yourself.

Table Manners and Etiquette
- All the previously written guidelines still count.

Social Events
- Do not talk about private topics in public.
- Do not make rude gestures in public.
- Do not ask personal questions.
- Do not speak rude language in public.
- Do not come late for social appointments.
- Do not leave large amounts of food on your plate; you'll offend the host.
- Do not leave the table before your host does.

  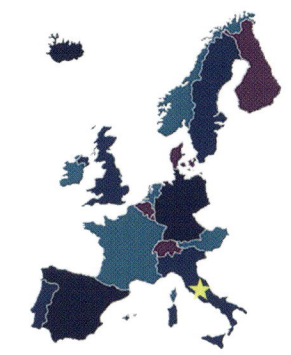

Italy - ITALIA

In General
Bordered by France, Switzerland, Austria and Slovenia in the north, and surrounded by the Mediterranean to the west and the Adriatic Sea to the east, Italy (its capital is Rome) and its isles, Sardinia, Elba, and Sicily, has it all.

"*La dolce vita*" [the sweet life]: great climate, popes, world-renowned artists, pasta, political chaos, great wine, fashion, music, and great cars. Its dreamy landscapes seem to be made for romance, and its three millennia of history, culture, and cuisine seduce just about everyone.
Who doesn't dream of being dressed in Armani suits, driving a Ferrari, listening to Verdi, drinking Chianti, gazing at the splendors of the Tuscany hills, or floating in a gondola on the Venetian canals?

A Little History
The first Roman republic was founded in 509 B.C. The republic's defeat of Carthage and Hellenic Macedonia during the three Punic Wars cleared the way for ultimate expansion into Spain, Britain, North Africa and present-day Iraq. Meanwhile, the Romans started to create the infrastructure of civilization: roads, aqueducts, cities, etc., and many of those still exist.

In 313 the empire's capital moved from Rome to Constantinople. The rise of cities and a merchant class culminated in the Renaissance of the 15th century. Painters, architects, poets, philosophers, and sculptors produced works of genius. Spain and then Austria invaded the empire and controlled the peninsula during the ensuing centuries, followed briefly by Napoleon's imperial period. The kingdom of Italy was declared in 1861. But there were already major cultural and social differences, which split the industrialized north from the poverty-stricken south.

Italy muddled through WWI, and when the second World War started, the king, during a severe Alzheimer's attack, asked one Benito Mussolini to take the reins of government under the auspices of his Fascist Party, which had a disastrous impact on the country. The postwar years were colored by extremism: extreme violence of terrorists, extreme center-right politics, extreme economic boom and economic crisis, extreme corruption and bribery in high places, and extremely cynical and tired people.

Italy's parliament has a reputation for scandal and resignation, and at times it has left Italy virtually ungoverned and utterly chaotic. No matter what, the country remains beautiful and never seems to stop producing more beauty than any other country in Europe.

Business Profile

Northern Italians are typically different than their southern countrymen. Because most of the industries are situated in the northern part of the country, the following will describe the ways of northern Italian businesspeople. They are charming, creative and they show great respect for traditions, their country's beauty, and artistic expressions.

However, they have their own way of doing business. Appointments should not necessarily be kept: "*domani*" [tomorrow] is always another day and a possibility.
They love to flirt with everything and everybody. But they adhere to a classic, steep, southern-European hierarchical style, with absolute authority in the hands of superiors.

Italians like to dress extremely elegantly, showing all the taste and class of the current trends. Family connections are important and useful. They expect foreigners to speak at least a little bit of Italian.
They express themselves in many words and ways. In other words, they love to talk using their hands, and all kinds of body language in order to show you what they mean, no matter how chaotic it may seem.

Even their agendas are chaotic. They like to introduce topics at random, and can re-discuss points that you thought, were already settled. Showing emotions is required in business meetings, signifying involvement.
Often, more than one person will be speaking at the same time, overlapping other discussion points. Northern business hours are usually 8:30 a.m. to 12:30 p.m. and 3:30 p.m. to 6:30 p.m. Larger companies usually work from 8:30 a.m. or 9:00 a.m. until 6:00 p.m. or 6:30 p.m., with at least one hour or so for lunch. This lunch break will be significantly longer, when eating out at a restaurant.

In central and southern Italy, business hours are from 8:30 a.m. to 12:45 p.m. then 4:30 p.m or 5:00 p.m. to 7:30 p.m.or 8:00 p.m. The southern business pace is usually less intense. In many cities, such as Rome, there is a long break lasting as long as two hours, from 1:30 p.m. to 3:30 p.m. Many business deals will be settled over great meals. Most firms are closed in August.

Italians treat their business opponents with charm and expect the same behavior from them. That doesn't mean, that you have to embrace, kiss and hug them right back if they do that to you.

First Business Encounters
- Give at least one or two months' notice for an appointment, but don't expect a fast reply.
- Be prepared to wait 15 to 45 minutes before your Italian counterpart appears or lets you into his or her office.
- Italians prefer to do business with a superficial acquaintance rather than a stranger; try to have a well-connected contact, who can make the right introductions for you.
- The best times to plan appointments are between 10:00 and 11:00 a.m., and after 3:00 p.m.
- Most Italians do not speak English very well, so you will probably need an interpreter in business situations. If your Italian counterpart does speak reasonable English it is worth ensuring that your presentation materials and discussions are kept clear and simple.
- Follow Italian business protocol by waiting until you are invited before using first names. You are expected to use "*Signore*" [Mr.] and "*Signora*" [Mrs.], plus the family name, when being introduced.
- Offer a short firm handshake as you make brief eye contact.
- Shake hands with everyone, when you are being introduced and when you are leaving.
- Tell people your first name and family name.
- Italians like to hear about your trip upon arrival, and expect compliments about their country. Especially since they became World Champion Soccer 2006 in Germany, where they defeated France in the final game.

Dress Code
- Bring formal, and if possible, elegant outfits as well as nice-looking casual ones. Dressing well is a priority here. Your clothing will be perceived as a reflection of your social standing and success, as well as your competence as a businessperson. Dress tastefully and stylishly.
- It is hard to "out-style" the Italians, especially the Milanese, because Milan is considered to be the very center of the fashion and design world.
- Men should wear expensive, sophisticated ties and well-cut dark suits and accessories such as cuff links, tie clips, and stylish watches.
- Women are advised to dress simply and with elegance. Accessorizing is also widely practiced here. Italian businesswomen usually wear more makeup and jewelry than other Europeans do.
- Perfumes and colognes are frequently used by both men and women.

Addressing people
- Italians like their titles. Try to remember them and if you are not sure, it is always better to address them with a title than without one.
- First-name basis is not very common in business environments.
- A male university graduate is given the title of "*Dottore,*" while the female equivalent is "*Dottoressa.*"
- Italian business etiquette requires that personal and professional titles are being used constantly, whether in casual conversation or formal writing.

Business Cards
- Bring enough cards. Italians love them.
- Make sure your card is in English and Italian and provides your title(s) and position.
- Pay special attention to the cards they give you, so you know who is who, and you also might want to compliment them on theirs.

Incentives
- Do not give gifts until you have received one.
- Gifts are expected for social events, especially to express your thanks after you have been invited to a dinner party at a home.
- Gifts are opened at the time they are given and received.
- Your gift should be a well-known brand name, that is, at the same time, small and not extravagant.
- Alcohol or crafts from your own country are good choices.

Doing Business
- For the first meeting, you need a simple and very clear, well-structured presentation.
- Do arrive at the bargaining table willing to negotiate, and remain flexible regarding legal and contractual obligations.
- Italians love to talk about everything but the agenda; be prepared for long meetings.
- Italians are not good at keeping promises. Be patient with them.
- When you make statements, make sure you can prove them to be true.
- Avoid boasting about your company, products, or yourself; Italians will do that for you.
- Most decisions are made in "closed quarters" by various people, not just the highest figure in authority. But in family-owned businesses, the head of the family usually makes the final decision.
- Final decisions are slow and protracted, usually taking several months.
- Italians will sometimes make sudden, unexpected demands as a way of unsettling the other side. The use of this strategy does not automatically mean the negotiations will collapse.

Business Meals
- Lunch and dinner are both excellent opportunities for business discussions.
- Italians love to eat and do business at the same time.
- Lunches will often be used for extended discussions and may take several hours. Typically, lunch will include a light starter, followed by soup, pasta, then meat or fish with vegetables, or a side salad. The meal finishes with dessert or cheese with fruit, and coffee.
- Wine and water are served throughout lunch, along with bread. Sometimes olive oil is used as a substitute for butter. Avoid mopping up any olive oil or sauce from your main plate with your bread.
- Dinner parties or large lunches often start with an aperitif such as Campari. One popular after-dinner drink is the very strong Grappa; another is Sambuca, a potent anise-flavored drink.
- A common toast is, "*cin cin*" or "*salute*".
- Italians sip their wine slowly. Drinking too much at once or appearing drunk, is considered an insult to Italian business etiquette.
- Expect dinners to start around 8:00 p.m. and last at least until midnight.
- Upscale restaurants expect men and women to dress very well.

Table Manners and Etiquette
- All the previous written guidelines are acknowledged in Italy, with one exception: You may use your fork by itself (in your right hand) when twirling pasta around it.

Social Events
- On the street, jeans and sneakers can be acceptable leisure wear.
- Keep conversation general. Try culture, music, sports (soccer) etc., for topics.
- Gifts are normal for social events. If you bring flowers, don't bring roses or chrysanthemums, and bring an odd number of them.
- When you receive an invitation stating "informal" dress, it really means tastefully coordinated clothes, sometimes including a jacket and tie for men.
- An invitation stating "formal" dress usually means formal evening wear, which is very dressy by American and Northern European standards.

First Business Encounters
- Never be late, not even one minute.
- Do not forget to mention their titles.
- Do not forget to give them compliments.

Dress Code
- Do not wear casual clothes for business appointments.

Addressing People
- Do not treat any person differently from another.

Business Cards
- Do not forget to have your card in English and Italian.

Incentives
- Do not bring a gift for the first meeting.

Doing Business
- Do not abruptly change the time and place for appointments.
- Do not expect "strictly business" talk.
- Do not feel intimidated by their hot temper; it's part of their show.
- Do not forget to close doors when you leave.

Business Meals
- Do not mop up any olive oil or sauce from your main plate with your bread.
- Do not refuse an invitation for a meal. Italians consider that to be an insult.
- Do not drink too fast.
- Do not break eye contact during the toast.
- Do not ask for liquor if your host doesn't offer it to you.

Table Manners and Etiquette
- All the previously written guidelines still count.

Social Events
- Do not chew gum in restaurants or on the street.
- Do not wear shorts in public. Also, you will not be admitted into a church wearing shorts, a sundress, or even a sleeveless top.
- Do not ask personal questions, or speak rude language in public.
- Do not come late for social appointments.
- Do not leave food on your plate; you will offend the host.
- Do not leave the table before your host does.

Spain - ESPAGNA

In General
Spain (its capital is Madrid) is located at the Iberian Peninsula together with Portugal, which is its neighbor on the west side. In the north Spain borders France and Andorra, with the Pyrenees as a natural barrier. The Balearic Islands (Mallorca, Menorca, and Ibiza) in the Mediterranean Sea, the Canary Islands in the Atlantic Ocean close to the Moroccan coast, and Ceuta and Melilla, located in northern Africa, are also Spanish territory. Spain has three climatic types: continental, maritime, and Mediterranean. It is the home of some of the world's great artists such as El Greco, Velázquez, Goya, Picasso and Dali.

One of Spain's better-known figures must be the 17th century's Don Quijote de La Mancha (created by Miguel Cervantes), who fought windmills and left a smile on the faces of many literature lovers. Today you can still enjoy the beautiful flamenco guitar music and the colorfully dressed dancers.

A Little History
The Romans arrived in the 3rd century B.C., but it took them two centuries to subdue the peninsula. By 714, the Muslim armies had occupied the entire peninsula, apart from the mountainous regions of northern Spain. The Muslim occupation of southern Spain lasted almost 800 years.

By the end of the 13th century, Castilla and Aragón had emerged as Spain's two main powers, and in 1469 these two kingdoms were united. Spain developed an enormous empire in the New World: the Americas. From Mexico to Peru, from Cuba to Bolivia, Spanish conquistadores are remembered there, not necessarily in a nice way, though.

Spain became one of the most powerful nations on earth.
The Spanish-American War of 1898 marked the end of the Spanish Empire. In 1931 the second republic of Spain was declared. In July 1936 the army overthrew the government.

By 1939, the Nationalists, led by Franco, won the civil war. About 100,000 Republicans were executed or died in prison after the war. Franco's 35-year dictatorship saw Spain isolated by economic blockades, excluded from NATO and the UN, and crippled by economic recession.

It wasn't until the early 1950s, that the country began to recover. By the 1970s, Spain had the fastest-growing economy in Europe. The only major bad thing on the domestic front since has been the terrorist campaign from the separatist militant group ETA, which is trying to secure an independent Basque homeland. In 1986 Spain joined the EU, and in 1992 Spain returned to the world stage, with Barcelona hosting the Olympic games. However, many people still frown on the cruel bull-fights.

Business Profile

Honor and personal pride are most important in their culture. Be aware of the differences in regional cultures.

In the Spanish business culture, hierarchy and position play an important role. Only the boss (popularly known as *el jefe or el padro*) has the authority to make decisions.

Subordinates are required to respect authority, to follow orders, and to deal with problems in such a way that they do not come to the attention of their superiors. They work well in teams, but suffer from a "closed-door" approach to management. Personal contacts and relationships are essential for all business success in Spain. Most Spaniards will seek the support and approval of family, friends, and colleagues before acting on their own.

There seems to be an underlying belief that a person is not a part of society, unless he or she is recognized as part of a group. In Madrid, Barcelona or Valencia, the working day means, arriving at the office around 9:00 a.m.

For many, the day will begin with drinking coffee and catching up with the news or office gossip. Work does not really start until 9:30 a.m. or 10:00 a.m., and the *siesta* remains an integral feature of the Spanish way of life. Therefore, if the working day includes dinner it may extend beyond midnight.

First Business Encounters
- Give at least one or two weeks' notice for an appointment made by telephone; allow at least a month for an appointment made by mail.
- Spaniards like to become acquainted with you before proceeding with business, so be accommodating and answer any questions about your background and family life.
- Knowledge of the language is essential.
- Spanish business introductions consist of exchanging cards, names, etc.
- Bring plenty of literature about your company.
- It helps to bring samples of your products and/or demonstrations of your service.
- Offer a firm handshake as you make brief eye contact.
- Shake hands with everyone, coming and going.
- Tell people your first name and family name when being introduced.
- Try to adjust to their ways. This demonstrates your respect for their culture, and also tells them that you are flexible.
- The Spanish like to hear about your trip upon arrival; tell them how it went.

Dress Code
- Bring formal and, if possible, elegant outfits as well as nice-looking casual ones. Dressing well, is a priority here. Your clothing will be perceived as a reflection of your social standing and success, as well as your competence as a businessperson, so, dress tastefully and stylishly.
- Men should wear well-cut dark suits, preferably with starched white shirts, nice ties, and accessories.
- Women are advised to dress simply and with elegance. Accessorizing is also widely practiced here. Spanish businesswomen usually wear more makeup and jewelry than other Europeans do.
- Perfumes and colognes are frequently used by both men and women.

Addressing People
- Businessmen or other professionals often use the courtesy title "*Don.*"
- It is important to address individuals by any titles they may have, followed by their surnames. For example, teachers prefer the title: "*profesor*", and engineers are referred to as: "*ingeniero.*"
- The Spanish like to be addressed the proper way. When addressing Spanish executives, basic titles of courtesy (followed by a surname) are always appropriate: sir = *señor*; madam = *señora*; miss = *señorita*.
- First-name basis is not very common in business environments.
- When you speak Spanish, address others by using the formal "*usted*" [formal you] unless you have been invited to use the more informal "*tu*" [informal you].
- Pay attention to distinct characteristics of Castilian, Galician, Basque, Catalan, Asturian and Andalusian cultures.

Business Cards
- Bring enough cards, with one side printed in English and the other in Spanish. Present your card with the Spanish side facing up.
- Make sure your card provides your title(s) and position.
- Pay special attention to the cards they give you, and you also might want to compliment them on theirs.

Incentives
- Gifts are usually given at the conclusion of successful negotiations.

Doing Business

- Spaniards are not particularly punctual; the agenda plays little role in meetings.
- They are philosophers and an oratorical style characterizes their communication, therefore patience is essential in all dealings with the Spanish.
- Their managers expect and show power and force.
- Be prepared to bargain; don't put your final price on the table in the beginning.
- Remember: maintaining pride and dignity is more important than time, money or practical considerations.
- You should try to remain warm and personal during negotiations while retaining your dignity, courtesy, and diplomacy.

- Avoid boasting about your company, products, or yourself; you'd better tell them how much you have suffered before you reached your present position.

Business Meals
- Business can be conducted over meals, but Spaniards regard eating as a primarily sociable activity. Financial matters have no place at table.
- Breakfast meetings are not very popular.
- Going out for coffee, lunch, "*tapas*" [delicious small bites of fresh food], or dinner is a vital ingredient to socializing, but not the time for doing business.
- If you invite your Spanish counterparts for dinner, choose an excellent restaurant.
- You should discuss business only if your Spanish companions initiate it.
- The host or hostess simply raises his or her glass and says, "*Salud.*" Guests do the same in response, and then you may start eating.
- Upscale restaurants expect men and women to dress very well.
- The person who extends the invitation pays the bill.
- If you have been invited out, you should reciprocate at a later date.

Table Manners and Etiquette
- All the previous written guidelines are acknowledged in Spain.

Social Events
- When walking on the street, informal dress is okay.
- For a social gathering, informal means nice casual clothes.
- Keep conversation general. Try food, sports, art, etc., for topics. Making fun of the French and the Germans is very popular.
- More-precious gifts are appreciated, when you are staying at a family's house.

First Business Encounters
- Do not come late.
- Do not be surprised if you are kept waiting for some 15 to 30 minutes.
- Do not forget to mention their titles.
- Do not be embarrassed by their personal questions.

Dress Code
- Do not wear casual clothes for business appointments.

Addressing People
- Do not forget to shake hands with everyone.
- Do not talk about the Basque movement, ETA.

Business Cards
- Do not forget to have your card in English and Spanish.

Incentives
- Do not bring a gift for the first encounter.

Doing Business
- Do not be discouraged by their "*mañana*" [tomorrow] attitude.
- Do not get infuriated by their bureaucracy.
- Do not forget to bargain.
- Do not feel intimidated by all their small talk; they want to get to know you.

Business Meals
- Do not start drinking until the host or hostess has proposed a toast.
- Do not break eye contact during the toast.
- Do not presume to seat yourself.
- Do not expect smoke-free restaurants.
- Do not think you'll get enough sleep; dinners go on until after midnight.

Table Manners and Etiquette
- All the previously written guidelines still count.

Social Events
- Do not show up on time for social events; take 30 minutes extra to arrive.
- Do not speak rude language in public.
- Do not bring dahlias, chrysanthemums, white lilies, or red roses.
- Do not leave large amounts of food on your plate; you will offend the host.
- Do not leave the table before your host does.
- Do not leave right away after dinner.

Portugal - PORTUGAL

In General
The Portuguese republic (its capital is Lisbon) has only one country for a neighbor: Spain on the east and north side. To the west and south it is surrounded by the waters of the Atlantic Ocean; therefore, it has a mainly maritime temperate climate. Maybe that is also the reason why Portugal has a rich seafaring past. The country is generally warm from April to October, though somewhat less so in the north, while the southern region of Algarve can experience very hot temperatures in midsummer. During winter, the north receives plenty of rain and temperatures can be chilly. The nation's best-known musical form is the melancholic *fado*, made world famous by Amalia Rodriguez. Another world-famous product of Portugal is their tasty after-dinner wine called: *Port*. The autonomous regions of Portugal are the isles Madeira (known for its Madeira wine) and Porto Santo, as well as the Azores, situated on the northwest side of the African coast.

A Little History
Portugal's history goes back to the Celts, who settled the Iberian Peninsula around 700 B.C. The region soon attracted many people and was colonized by the Phoenicians, Greeks, Romans, and the Visigoths in the 6th century. Not long after that, Portugal was taken over by the Muslim state Cordoba. This, then-Christian state defeated Cordoba one more time and gained all the territories of which it consists today. In the 15th and 16th century, Portugal became one of the leading exploring countries in Europe. It established colonies in South America, Africa, and Asia. Portugal was united with and subordinated to Spain in a personal union between 1580 and 1640. Independence was regained in 1640, and Portugal continued as a kingdom until 1910, when the monarchy was expelled and the first republic established. Portugal is now a democratic republic in the EU.

Business Profile
The businesses are characterized by their strong hierarchy: heavy and structured, superiors expect to be obeyed, and subordinates expect explicit and direct instructions. Little independent action will be taken without direct orders. Management style is paternal rather than dictatorial, and conflict is avoided. Personal relationships are essential to doing business successfully.

The Portuguese businesspersons show flexibility, warmth, and friendliness toward their counterparts. Like in many southern European countries family and personal contacts, relationships, and networks are extremely important.

Business communication style is personal, eloquent, and emotional. They are also keen negotiators, and place great importance on written communication, possibly in an effort to avoid uncertainty and ambiguity. They are often called Europe's most-skilled negotiators. They negotiate in small teams and are friendly and charming.

They may "play dumb" to silence the suspicion of their adversaries. It is not unusual for them to change course dramatically during negotiations, or to introduce a wildly unacceptable request to unnerve their opponents. They don't have respect for deadlines. Their meetings are badly run and inconclusive. Their customer focus is very blurred.
Friends and family come first. They suffer from a large, inefficient bureaucracy, mainly because of its disorganization and their rule-breaking.

However, the Portuguese treat their business opponents with warmth and respect, and expect the same behavior from them. Here is what you may and may not do in order to smooth the path toward doing business successfully. None of the ideas hereafter are absolute guides to all situations and people in Portugal. There are considerable differences between generations, regions, and crucially, the relative depth of their contacts with other business cultures (especially yours). Expect the unexpected.

First Business Encounters
- Give at least one weeks' notice for an appointment and confirm this two days before the set date.
- Punctuality is not very important; you may arrive 5 to 15 minutes late.
- Be patient.
- Don't be surprised, if they keep you waiting up until 30 minutes.
- Business introductions consist of exchanging cards, names, etc.
- Offer a handshake, as you make brief eye contact.
- Always shake hands with everyone, coming and going.
- Tell people your first name and family name, when being introduced.

Dress Code
- Check the weather report of the country.
- Bring formal outfits as well as casual ones.
- Men wear suits and ties; women wear fashionable suits or skirts.
- Long-sleeved shirts/blouses are important, especially for men.
- The Portuguese like to be dressed the "trendy" right way, but still a bit conservatively.

Addressing People
- They don't insist on their titles, but they do take pride in them. Their titles are too complicated for foreigners to even begin to understand and pronounce.
- First-name basis is not very common in business environments.
- Compliment the country, food, city, climate, wine, and soccer to stay on their safe side.

Business Cards
- Bring enough cards. They like them.
- Make sure your card is in English and provides your title(s) and position, for they have a deep respect for academic degrees.
- Pay special attention to the cards they give you, and compliment them on theirs.

Incentives
- It is common to bring a gift to a prospective business partner.
- Bring something nice from your home country.

Doing Business

- For the first meeting you don't need a well-prepared agenda, but you do need a very clear, well-structured presentation.
- Take good meeting notes and offer to do minutes, if there are any.
- You really must have a lot of patience with them. Dialogue is important.
- Consensus rather than "winner/loser" tends to be the underlying philosophy.
- They tend to analyze their personal interest in an action or deal.
- Understanding hidden agendas is an important skill, you should have.
- Portuguese businesspeople are experts at dealing with last-minute crisis.
- They respect qualities such as honesty and straightforwardness.

Business Meals

- Lunch is a key business activity; but don't start talking business before dessert.
- Dinner is mainly for entertainment; don't talk about business unless your host starts.
- The Portuguese will usually try to pay for a foreign guest's meal as part of the culture of hospitality.
- Upscale restaurants expect men and women to dress very well.
- Reciprocate their lavish and generous hospitality.

Table Manners and Etiquette

- All the previous written guidelines are acknowledged in Portugal.

Social Events

- When walking on the street, informal dress is okay.
- For a social gathering, informal means nice casual clothes.
- Keep conversation general. Try culture, soccer, art, etc., for topics.
- Gifts are acceptable for social events. If you bring flowers, don't bring roses.
- More-precious gifts are appreciated, when you are staying at a family's house.
- If you're invited to a *Fado restaurant*, where the traditional *Fado* music is performed, know that you can not have extensive conversation, as it is very rude to talk while the singing is going on.

First Business Encounters
- Do not forget to mention their titles.
- Do not get aggravated when they make you wait.

Dress Code
- Do not wear casual clothes for business appointments.
- Do not overdress by wearing flashy designer clothes and jewelry.

Addressing People
- Do not treat any person differently from another.
- Do not forget to shake hands with everyone.
- Do not make comparisons between Portugal and Spain or France.

Business Cards
- Do not forget to have your card in English.

Incentives
- Do not expect gifts in return.
- Don't bring wine; the Portuguese believe they make the best wine themselves.

Doing business
- Do not abruptly change the time and place for appointments.
- Do not get furious when things take longer than you want them to.
- Do not feel intimidated by all their titles; it's part of their heritage.
- Do not ever write anything in red ink, not even small notes, checks, etc.
- Do not launch straight into the negotiation; take time for small talk.
- Do not accept statements, verbal or written, as true.

Business Meals
- Do not use dinners for business meetings.
- Do not talk business before your host does.
- Do not presume to seat yourself.

Table Manners and Etiquette
- All the previously written guidelines still count, but the Portuguese treat them in a very relaxed manner.

Social Events
- Do not speak rude language in public.
- Do not stretch in public.
- Do not turn your back toward someone in the group you're with.
- Do not arrive at the set time for social appointments.
- Do not leave large amounts of food on your plate; you will offend the host.
- Do not leave the table before your host does.

The Waiters

An airline executive from **Singapore** on a negotiation mission in **Portugal** wondered about the way the waiters were serving him during a business dinner. "Is this normal?" he asked. "They confuse me; serving me from the right, then from the left, then coming to take away plates, and putting back new silverware. They make me feel rather uncomfortable."

In general, it is like this. Only when the waiters have to serve from a bowl or a bigger dish, do they come from the left side. All other actions, such as taking away plates, changing silverware, pouring drinks, etc., will be on your right side. In the restaurant business, hygiene is very important, and because most of the waiters are right handed, they would have to bend over the food in order to serve it on your plate. That is why sometimes they come to your left side.

Bibliography

Book
Zakelijke etiquette, de sleutel tot success; Magda Berman
(Business etiquette, the key to success)

Internet sites
www.neia.org
www.europa.eu.int
www.worldbiz.com
www.geocities.com
www.cyborlink.com
www.atn-riae.agr.ca
www.lonelyplanet.com
www.encyclopedia.com
www.eurograduate.com
www.kwintessential.co.uk
www.executiveplanet.com
www.appliedlanguage.com
www.businesstravelogue.com
www.workabroad.monster.com

Lay out and designs ©®
Inside Out USA
t +1 678 2837874 • email kstenbroeke@gmail.com
Scope Communicatie, Heemstede, The Netherlands
t +31 23 5244112 • email scopeaer@wxs.nl

Illustrations
Courtesy of Microsoft Clipart
google.freeclipart.com
free-clip-art.net

Printed in the United States
60223LVS00001B